CYCLE WORLD

RIDING SKILLS

TIPS FOR EVERY MOTORCYCLIST

D1468510

CYCLE WORLD

RIDING SKILLS

TIPS FOR EVERY MOTORCYCLIST

MARK LINDEMANN

weldon**owen**

CONTENTS

1 START OUT RIGHT

In the bad old days, we learned to ride a motorcycle without much professional input: We just stumbled into it with no real instruction, thrashed around awkwardly, tried to avoid disaster, and counted ourselves lucky if we could hang on for more than a couple of minutes. Today, though, there are much better ways. Here are some good places to start.

THE MOTOR VEHICLE DEPARTMENT In most countries you need some sort of license. That motor vehicle department is also a good place to ask about rider-training resources. If nothing else, they usually have literature telling you what to expect on the test.

MANUFACTURERS Every major motorcycle manufacturer has a website, and most of them have links to rider-training information. It doesn't matter which brand you start with, although some will offer free or discounted training courses if you purchase one of their bikes.

A DEALER Your local dealers probably won't offer training, but may know who does in your area.

YOUR LOCAL AUTOMOBILE CLUB Clubs like the American Automobile Association ("Triple A") in America, the AA or RAC in the UK, the ADAC in Germany, and many more often cater to motorcyclists as well as auto drivers. Invariably they can steer you towards insurance, licensing, and training solutions.

2 GET YOUR LICENSE

Motorcycle laws vary greatly from place to place, but one truth is very evident: Unlicensed riders are more likely to be involved in an accident. You may have difficulty getting insurance without a license, too.

Start by visiting your local Department of Motor Vehicles, either online or in person. Find out whether your local laws require you to take a written test, a riding test, or both. While you're there (or on the website), determine whether they have any pre-test materials you can study—they often do, at no charge.

Find out if there's any specific training you will need before you take the test, and what equipment you need to have for the test: helmet, gloves, boots, jacket, and/or a bike? Also, inquire with the DMV whether attending a certified riding school can substitute for all or part of the test.

Study the laws, and take rider training if you decide this is right for you (it is). Practice your skills, especially low-speed maneuvering and, when you're ready, go for it.

3 FIND A RIDING SCHOOL

Motorcycle riding schools fall into several categories. Make sure you pick the right one for your skill level.

BASIC RIDER LICENSING AND TRAINING This instruction is the most common. It'll take you from zero to applying for your license. Most of the time these classes are geared for streetbike riders. Very often they will provide all the safety equipment you need—and a bike as well.

ADVANCED RIDER TRAINING These schools are for street riders who want to advance their skills to the next level. They can be operated either by the same foundations that set up the basic schools, or they can be offered on racetracks by various expert riders.

RACING ASSOCIATION SCHOOLS Many racing associations will require you to take one of their school courses before you can participate in an event.

These classes are often held at your local racetrack. You'll need your own equipment and a track-prepped bike.

RACING SCHOOLS Separate from the association schools, these are often run by former racers who either tour the country or operate out of a home track. The classes can last several days and are often a nice vacation opportunity for advanced riders: You can meet a famous racer, hang out with him for a couple of days, and get first-hand riding tips—and lots of track time on a new course.

DIRTBIKE SCHOOLS These courses can be either basic or advanced. Like the roadbike schools, you may want to pick one at an exotic location and make a vacation out of it. This training is becoming more and more popular for the big twin-cylinder adventure bikes like the BMW GS series and the KTMs. Your dealership can probably give you a good idea of what's out there.

4 LEARN FROM EVERY RIDE

The first key to learning from a ride is to do something different. If you normally ride city streets, try riding in the canyons. Or in the dirt. Or in another country.

And even that five-day-a-week commute is an opportunity to hone your skills. On Monday, practice your braking. Tuesdays, look farther ahead. Wednesdays, concentrate on your footwork, weighting the pegs in turns. Thursdays, practice smoothness. Fridays, countersteering. And on the weekend, put it all together.

An athlete does pushups and sit-ups not to become pushup champion, but to become more fit overall. Think of your riding the same way.

5 PERFORM A PRE-RIDE CHECK

Pilots perform a walk-around (a visual and mechanical inspection of the aircraft) every time they fly. You should as well—it's called a pre-ride check, it'll take just a minute, and it might save your life. Here's what to look for.

☐ **TIRES** Check visually first, looking for excessive damage, wear, or nails in treads or sidewalls; check pressure with a gauge at least weekly.

☐ **RIMS** Especially on dirtbikes and dual-sports, inspect the spokes to make sure none are broken. Run a wrench or screwdriver over the spokes—this will emit a tone, and a loose spoke will sound different.

☐ **LEAKS** Your bike shouldn't be leaking oil, coolant, fuel, or brake fluid.

☐ **THROTTLE** It should operate smoothly, without binding, and fully close under its own power.

☐ **BRAKES** Pull the brake lever and depress the pedal to check that the brakes are operating as they should.

☐ **LIGHTS** Make sure the brake, taillight, headlight, and indicators work right.

☐ **ENGINE OIL** Check the oil level and add more if necessary.

☐ **FUEL LEVEL** Obviously.

☐ **DRIVE CHAIN** Check condition, tension, and lubrication.

☐ **CLUTCH** Check for smooth operation.

☐ **CABLES** Check for loose control cables.

☐ **NUTS AND BOLTS** See if anything has vibrated loose, especially before and after dirtbike rides. Give a light tug with a wrench on any known problem nuts and bolts, especially the ones in the exhaust system.

6 BREAK IN AN ENGINE

From "ride it like you stole it" to "you can ruin your engine in the first hour if you're not careful," you'll hear more superstition and voodoo around engine break-in protocol than just about any other aspect of owning a motorcycle. Most riders want their engine to have a long life, produce good power, and not burn oil. Here's what to do to make sure that happens.

MIX IT UP Avoid operating the bike at a droning, constant rpm for the first several hundred miles or kilometers. Speed up, slow down, and repeat—this exercise will create both positive and negative pressure in the combustion chamber, and especially on the rings. These alternating forces help create a good ring seal, which boosts power and cuts down on engine oil consumption.

EASE INTO REVS Don't over-rev the engine, but don't under-rev it either. A pretty good rule of thumb is to take it up to 50 percent of redline for the first 50 miles (80 km), and then up to 75 percent for the next several hundred. Practice this in turn with the alternate on/off power and load technique we've already discussed.

KEEP IT UP Never neglect routine maintenance. Many bikes will call for an initial inspection after 600 miles (965 km): adjusting the chain, setting the valves, changing the oil. Do it all—especially the oil and filter. In the first few hours of operation, the engine will produce tiny metal shavings as the parts wear in, and all that metal ends up in your oil and filter. Pull the plug and get that junk out of there.

7 KNOW YOUR TRANSMISSION

The best way to understand how your motorcycle's transmission works is to ride a bicycle. Why? On a bicycle, you are the engine, you feel how the load on the engine changes as you shift gears.

Motorcycle transmissions (the most common manual-shift kind) use pairs of gears moving laterally on a pair of shafts to change the ratios between the engine and the rear wheel. Pushing the foot-shift lever pushes or pulls these gear pairs into or out of engagement. Here are some of the principal parts, and what they do.

PRIMARY DRIVE Power from the engine's crankshaft flows into the engine through these gears or chain.

CLUTCH Couples or uncouples engine power to input shaft.

SHIFT LEVER Used to change gears.

SHIFT DRUM Converts the up-and-down motion of the gear shifter to the shift fork's horizontal motion.

SHIFT FORK Moves gear pairs laterally in and out of engagement on shafts.

INPUT SHAFT Power flows through this shaft to a selected gear pair and then out through the countershaft.

GEARS Multiply force from the engine.

DOGS Gear pairs slide laterally on their shaft, and the dogs connect adjacent gear pairs.

OUTPUT OR COUNTERSHAFT The power-out shaft.

FINAL-DRIVE Chain or driveshaft that links the transmission to the rear wheel.

8 SHIFT WITHOUT THE CLUTCH

Sacrilege you say? Not with modern sportbikes and dirtbikes.

This is easiest at the higher gear ratio pairings, and at higher rpm. Because of the wide ratio jump from first to second, use the clutch for that shift, but after that it's fair game. Apply a bit of pressure under the shift lever. When ready, back off the throttle and snap the shifter up. Once you shift, quickly get on the throttle .

After mastering upshifting, you can downshift the same way. This is rare on streetbikes, but useful on a dirtbike.

9 KNOW YOUR BIKE'S LIMITS

If your bike has no tachometer, how do you know when to shift? Most modern bikes have rev limiters, so you won't over-rev your engine while in gear. But redlining for each shift is a bad idea.

UPSHIFTING For best fuel economy, shift early and often, operating at small throttle openings. Pay attention to your rpm decrease between shifts. As long as your next upshift doesn't drop the rpm in the next gear below idle, you'll be fine. For the most power and fastest times (and less economy), upshift at your bike's horsepower peak.

DOWNSHIFTING Downshifting slows your bike, or adjusts the engine's rpm to make more power. But for slowing, you have brakes. Instead, for an upcoming curve, brake in advance of the turn, anticipating what gear you'll need to use to exit the turn. As you're slowing, downshift the bike, releasing the clutch as you finish braking.

Sometimes it pays not to shift at all—like on a long uphill or downhill in the dirt. Bottom line? In the words of *Cycle World*'s Kevin Cameron, "When the bike quits lunging forward, it's time to shift."

10 IMPROVISE A CRUISE CONTROL

You're droning through the Russian steppes, on a road so straight you can see the curvature of the earth. And your wrist is killing you. What to do? With nothing more than a simple rubber band and a pencil or a popsicle stick, relief is on the way!

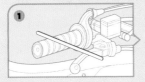

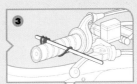

STEP 1 Place the stick over the throttle grip so that it's lying on top of your front-brake lever.

STEP 2 Loop one end of the rubber band over the front portion of the stick as shown.

STEP 3 Loop the other end of the rubber band over the rear portion of the stick, pulling it tight. Adjust tension with more wraps as needed.

STEP 4 Twist the throttle to the desired opening, and hold it in position.

STEP 5 Push the stick down so it contacts the top of the brake lever, and let go. We can't fully recommend this method, but your wrist will thank you for it.

11 BECOME A BETTER RIDER IN 12 STEPS

PAY ATTENTION Thoughts drifting as you ride? Park the bike, get a cup of coffee and get your mind right.

RIDE A DIRTBIKE You can learn a lot about traction and body positioning like a dirtbike. You'll also learn to deal with water or sand on paved roads.

RIDE BEHIND A BETTER RIDER Follow someone better; you'll see just how much you can still learn.

COMPETE Nobody wants to finish last. Competition at any level makes you focus and try harder.

LOOK FARTHER When we get lazy or tired, we look only a short distance in front of the bike. Lift your chin and look ahead. In turns, look through the turn, not just into the entrance.

SIT RIGHT Your body position makes a tremendous difference in how a motorcycle responds.

ADJUST YOUR CONTROLS Always check your controls, handlebars, and footpegs.

CLEAN AND MAINTAIN YOUR RIDE As you clean your bike, you can spot problems. And doing your own maintenance makes you more aware of your machine's overall condition.

RIDE IN THE RAIN You'll learn about traction, lean angle, steering input, braking, and overall smoothness.

RIDE ANOTHER BIKE A new machine makes you sharpen your focus and keeps you learning.

BE SMOOTH Pick a day of the week and forget about everything else but being smooth. Anticipate the road or trail and all of your inputs, to build awareness.

BRAKE HARD Don't wait for a panic stop to practice this one. In a safe area, practice hard stops using both the front and rear brakes.

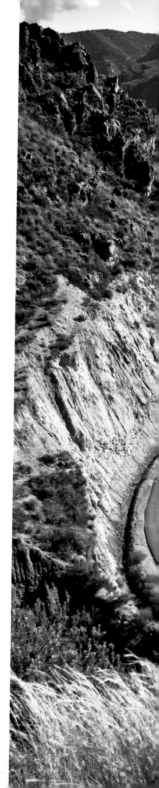

12 COUNTERSTEER CORRECTLY

Every rider knows that you lean when you turn. But few understand a critical aspect of this—countersteering.

Countersteering is the technique you consciously or unconsciously apply to initiate that lean. In short, you steer left to lean right, and vice versa. In order to fully understand the theory, you need to get your head around camber thrust, roll angle, and centripetal force. But to ride you only need to understand the practice.

To really get a feel for it, get going down a straight piece of road at a moderate speed—anything over 10 mph (16 kph). Open both your hands so only your palms are in contact and your fingers point straight up—so you can only push the bar, not pull. Now push with your right hand, and see what happens.

You'll experience a momentary dip to the left, and then the bike will bank slightly to the right. Combine countersteering with a quick weight shift to the inside footpeg, and *voilà*—your bike responds instantly.

Why is it so important to understand this? It can, literally be a matter of life and death. In a car, when we need to turn right to avoid an accident, we yank the wheel to the right. Doing that same thing on a bike does just the opposite—which can be deadly.

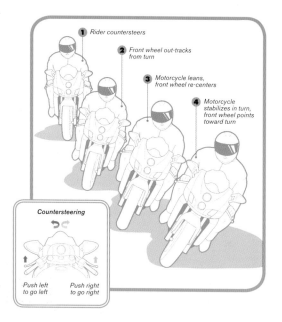

1. Rider countersteers
2. Front wheel out-tracks from turn
3. Motorcycle leans, front wheel re-centers
4. Motorcycle stabilizes in turn, front wheel points toward turn

Countersteering

Push left to go left · Push right to go right

13 DON'T GET (TANK) SLAPPED

Also known as the death wobble or speed shimmy, the tankslapper is a force to be reckoned with. The handlebars shake rapidly side-to-side, increasing in force and amplitude.

The baby tankslapper cycles back and forth two or three times, then goes away. A big one grows faster and stronger until you crash.

What causes it? Many factors: tire stiffness, forward weight transfer, road surface, and chassis stiffness. Wheelie your bike until the front wheel stops turning, land hard, and you'll often conjure one. The most common causes are exiting a bumpy corner or a sudden weight transfer.

What should you do? Don't let go. Stop doing whatever it was that brought it on. Easier said than done, but usually you should slide back on the seat and take some of the weight off the front end with the throttle.

The best method is to fit a steering damper—you'll seldom see a race bike without one.

14 MASTER TRAIL-BRAKING

Brakes aren't just for slowing down or stopping—they can also help you turn as well as settle your chassis.

Traditional riding instruction suggests braking with the bike straight up and down—before you turn. This technique is safe, but it's not the only way. Trail-braking means staying on the brakes through the turn entrance, or all the way to the apex. Brake less as the apex grows closer, then accelerate out of the turn. It's faster, and easier to tighten the radius towards the end of the turn if you need to avoid a problem.

You'll usually use both front and rear brakes. Another method involves lightly dragging the rear brake while you're on the gas. This settles the bike's chassis and to help it stand up on acceleration.

The secret with either technique is smoothness—easy on, easy off. Both are skills a rider should practice and master.

15 GO ENGINE BRAKING

Your motorcycle's engine gets you up to speed, but you can also use it to slow down. When you decelerate—coming to a stop, going into a turn, or on a long downhill that may roast your brake pads—your engine can save some wear and tear.

By rolling off the throttle while still in gear, the engine's compression does a good job of slowing down the bike. Downshifting increases that effect—and prepares you to accelerate again after slowing or stopping.

Your engine can be used to slow the bike as long as you do so safely: Don't engine-brake too quickly, or downshift through gears too fast, or from too high engine rpm. And don't be afraid to use the front and rear brakes as well, to give you greater braking power and finesse.

16 DON'T DISREGARD THE DOWNSHIFT

The primary reason you downshift is to keep the engine in its powerband for the given speed and situation. A second, less intuitive, reason is to utilize the engine's compression braking. With the throttle closed, the engine applies a steady braking force to the rear wheel, which is very useful on long downhills, especially off-road. When driving a car, you downshift to keep from burning up the brakes or boiling the brake fluid. On a bike, it's about maintaining traction and control.

17 TAKE THEM FOR A RIDE

Plenty of people are happy to tell anyone who will listen why riding is a bad idea. Most of them mean well, a few have an anti-bike agenda, and some are just plain ignorant. The easiest way to fight back? Offer a lot of rides to friends and family members.

You're not trying to get them hooked on bikes and turn them into riders—although that may happen, too. Just think of yourself as an ambassador. Even if that person never gets a license or buys a bike, they'll be more likely to look out for riders when they're driving, or to support a kid or significant other who wants a bike. Show them how much fun riding can be—get them outdoors and let them feel the wind and smell the trees. Show them what you already know—that bikes are all about freedom and fun.

18 MAKE A GREAT FIRST IMPRESSION

You want to make this fun for your passenger, right? First, make sure your bike's set up right. Plenty of air in the tires? More preload in the rear shock? Then be familiar with state laws in your area for carrying a passenger. Make sure he or she is dressed correctly and has a helmet. Pick a ride that's fun but not too long.

Before you start, talk through every step—how to get on the bike, where to sit, what to hang on to, how to lean with you. Start slow, and stay smooth—no sudden starts, stops, or direction changes. Pick a smooth line and watch for bumps. Take slow, wide turns. Leaning, especially at speed, freaks a passenger out more than anything else.

Take breaks so your passenger can relax, and take the chance to ask if he or she is comfortable. You may feel if your passenger is anxious before you hear it.

19 STAY DRY

Backpacking and other similar shops offer a variety of waterproofing treatments for leather and textile garments. Even if a jacket isn't totally waterproofed, the treatments make it easier to keep clean. Gore-Tex garments require special treatment; try an outdoors shop for those supples.

20 BE A GOOD PASSENGER

Most of the responsibility for the ride falls to the pilot, but as a passenger, you can help to ensure a good experience. Here's how.

DRESS FOR SUCCESS Wear what a smart rider wears: Long pants, sturdy over-the-ankle shoes, a long-sleeved jacket. Get a good-fitting helmet if the rider doesn't have a spare, and bring gloves that fit.

FIND YOUR FOOTING Almost every bike will have a set of passenger footpegs— if their location isn't obvious, ask the rider. Once you're on the bike, keep your feet on the pegs, even at stops. Also, watch for the exhaust pipes. If the bike's been running for a bit, they'll be hot enough to give you a bad burn.

GET ON FROM THE LEFT Let the rider get on first, so he can hold the bike stable before you climb on.

HANG ON Ask if you should hold onto the rider, their hips, handrails or seat straps, or place one hand in front of you and one hand behind.

LEAN WITH THE RIDER Motorcycles lean when they turn. If you lean the wrong way, you'll annoy the rider at best, and throw him or her off balance at worst. If the bike is turning right, look over the rider's right shoulder; for left turns, make it the left shoulder. When in doubt, keep your helmet in line with the rider's and you'll naturally follow him.

DON'T BE A HEADBANGER Anticipate when the rider will brake. When they do, your body will shift forward. Keep your helmet from banging into theirs. It's not dangerous, but it is annoying. You can support yourself by placing your hands on the fuel tank.

SPEAK UP If you're uncomfortable, say something, A frightened passenger tenses up and makes the rider uncomfortable. The bike becomes more difficult to handle, too. The best compliment a rider can pay to you is to say he didn't even know you were there.

21 RIDE SAFELY WITH JUNIOR

When is a child old enough to go for a ride? It's really less a matter of age and more about size and strength. Junior needs to be able to hold on securely and put his or her feet on the footpegs—you may need to improvise some peg extensions or blocks. And depending on your girth and the child's arm length, holding on around your waist may not be an option. A belt for you with handles the child can grip is a better option if your machine lacks handholds that are kid-friendly. Here are some other things to consider.

☐ Check all local and state laws and guidelines. Some regions restrict the age of a child passenger, or have other rules. This information should be easily available online; if not, call your local department of motor vehicles or other similar agency.

☐ Never carry a child in front of you.

☐ Make sure the child wears the same level of protective clothing as any other rider, especially a helmet and eye protection.

☐ Keep the rides short and fun. If a child falls asleep, you may not notice until he falls off.

☐ Choose a bike with a passenger backrest if possible.

☐ Make sure the child is mature enough to understand and obey instructions.

☐ Make sure the child is enjoying the ride. If you frighten him now with excessive speed or scary lean angles, he may dislike bikes forever.

☐ Provide positive feedback—take photos of your ride, tell them how well they did, and be sure to ask if they had fun.

22 ENCOURAGE KIDS TO RIDE

Kids are the future of motorcycling. Get them started early, and you're ensuring the future of the sport. Better still, riding is good, clean fun.

Riding a motorcycle is all about personal responsibility, and the sooner a kid learns about that concept, the happier he or she will be.

If you have a streetbike, put them on the passenger seat and take them for a ride. If they're old enough, getting them on their own dirtbike is even better.

And you know what? Someday when you're in the old-folks' home, that same kid may show up to visit you. Or better yet, spring you from that place for a couple of hours and take you for a ride. Ain't payback grand?

23 SPLIT LANES THE RIGHT WAY

Lane splitting, lane sharing, traffic filtering—whatever you call the practice, it's one of the advantages motorcycles offer over cars. Basically, it's riding between slow or stopped traffic lanes. It's legal in most of Europe and Asia. In the United States, it's legal in California (we hope other states will eventually get a clue). Here's how to do it safely.

BE AWARE Consider the environment. If you can't fit, don't split. Don't split next to large trucks or other high vehicles—you risk being knocked under their wheels. As you near a car, see if the driver is on the phone or texting.

BE SMART Split lanes only if traffic is slower than 30 miles per hour (48 kph). You won't have much room to maneuver; more speed mean you cover more ground, and thus have less time to react and brake.

PICK A LANE Typically, it's safer to split between the fast lane and the next-fastest. Look ahead, but not too far ahead. The car that's going to get you is the one next to you, or close ahead.

DON'T SPEED Never ride over 10 miles per hour (16 kph) faster than the moving traffic surrounding you. Consider running your bike a gear l ower than normal to take advantage of compression braking, and more responsive acceleration.

AVOID EXITS You've seen a distracted driver spot his exit at the last minute and swerve over four lanes of traffic—you don't want to be in his way.

STAY SOLO Don't split lanes when there's another motorcycle rider doing so nearby. Sometimes, when drivers see a bike moving their way, they move over as a courtesy. If they see the other bike first, they may get into your space.

BE READY Always cover your (front) brake lever and (rear) brake pedal.

BE NICE If a driver moves over to give you room, it's OK wave thanks. If a car doesn't move over, don't make obscene gestures. Who knows what he'll do to the next biker he sees if you anger him?

24 PLAY SAFELY IN TRAFFIC

Think road racing is dangerous? Those guys have it easy compared to your average urban commuter. The following tips can keep you alive.

CHOOSE YOUR ROUTE Look for a route that moves well and gives you room to maneuver.

MIND THE GUNK The crud that builds up on city streets can compromise your traction and ability to corner and stop. It'll be worst in the center of a lane, just before intersections, or if no rain has fallen recently.

LOOK AROUND Don't just gaze in front of you; look ahead and around. You should use your mirrors, but don't trust them alone.

PLAN YOUR ESCAPE What if that car ahead comes into your lane? What if something falls off that truck ahead of you? Where are you going to go? Always look for a way out.

KEEP MOVING Don't pull up so close to a car that you can't maneuver; if you're sitting still, you're a sitting duck.

STAND OUT Wear bright, reflective colors, use a headlight modulator (if legal in your area), and use your horn if you have to.

AVOID BLIND SPOTS If you can't see the driver's face in his mirrors, he can't see you, and that puts you in danger. Leave that blind spot ASAP.

KEEP CONTROL Keep your fingers on the front brake and clutch levers (and the horn button), and your foot over the rear brake.

BEWARE OF INTERSECTIONS Most motorcycle accidents involve a car violating the rider's right of way, especially turning left in front of him. And intersections are where people turn.

DON'T BLOCK EXITS Drivers swerve across lanes to exits in a big hurry sometimes. Riding between a car and a freeway exit is asking for trouble.

25 AVOID TARGET FIXATION

"Look where you want to go." Even a beginning rider course should teach you that, and it's sound advice no matter how much experience you gain. The bike will go where you're looking. If there's a pothole or debris in front of you, or a car pulls out, or an animal runs into your path, don't look directly at it—look for a way out.

Two corollaries: Look through the turn, not just at the apex. And second, don't look in front of you; look ahead of you. Flat-track riders call that shortness of vision "riding the front wheel." You'll never be safe if you're not looking far enough ahead.

26 USE YOUR RADAR, RIDER

In countless action-packed war flicks from World War II up to the modern age, you've seen the sweep-and-ping of navy sonar, or the same display on a radar console. Your bike may not have surface-to-surface missiles, but you can still apply the same concept to enhance your safety on the road.

The basic principle is to keep your eyes moving. Just like avoiding target fixation, look where you want to go, and look for a way out of potential (or clear and present) danger. But just like sonar or radar, once you're done surveying the area, start another sweep.

Your eyes move faster than almost any other part of your body, and you can quickly take in the details of the road and any potential obstacles in a literal blink of an eye. Sweep your field of vision near to you, then farther away, then farther still. Keep objects in mind, but don't fixate on them, and start your sweep again. A good rule of thumb is to do a full sweep of your field of vision every five to 15 seconds. Ping!

27 READ THE RADIUS

Increasing, decreasing, or constant radius—it sounds like a geometry class. Pay attention to this course; if you don't know how a turn is built, you'll end up with more than just a bad grade. If a turn curves around at the same rate the whole way through, it has a constant radius. You adjust your speed at the entry, and then you accelerate at the exit. Simple.

If the turn starts out sharp and then opens up wide, that's called an increasing radius, an even more forgiving turn.

But if a turn tightens in on itself—plenty of freeway offramps and mountain roads do so—this is called a decreasing radius. You'll need to lean hard if you get into one of these too fast, and that can push you to the edge of the road or over the midline. In decreasing radius turns, enter more slowly than normal, lean more, or ride a slightly wider line and apply throttle only when the remaining corner is fully seen. On unfamiliar roads, assume every turn is a decreasing radius.

28

READ THE CROWN

Paved roads are rarely flat; they usually slope to help water drain or to help a vehicle hold the road surface. The most common feature is the crown—a road higher in the center than the edges.

Since you lean a bike over when you turn, it's important to pay attention to the crown. On right turns, the crown works for you, but on left turns it works against you. (This presumes that you ride on the right; in the UK, Japan and countries where you ride on the left, the opposite holds true.) If you drift over onto the crown, your machine loses its cornering clearance very quickly. Sometimes the crown won't be in the center of the road at all.

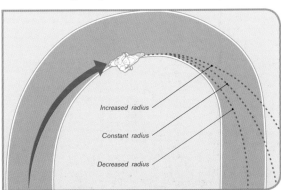

Increased radius

Constant radius

Decreased radius

29 FOIL BIKE THIEVES

There are few things worse than coming out of your home in the morning keys in hand, ready to ride and seeing . . . nothing. Motorcycle theft is all too common, but you can thwart those evil bastards. Here's how, in six easy steps.

KEEP IT OUT OF SIGHT If a thief can't see your bike, he can't decide to steal it. Parking your machine in a secure garage or shed, especially at night, is choice number one. Well, choice number two, really. A bank vault would be even better.

KEEP IT IN SIGHT On the road and need to stop for lunch? Park your bike by the restaurant window and sit right next to it. Or how about paying someone to watch it for you? Darkness is the bike thief's friend, so park in a well-lit area.

BE A KILLJOY Something as simple as a hidden kill switch can stop a bad guy from hot-wiring your ride. Even pulling a plug wire can stop the casual thief, or at least buy you time.

MAKE SOME NOISE Invest in an alarm, ideally one that also kills the ignition while it alerts you.

BOX IT IN A single bike sitting in a wide-open parking lot is just calling out to some bad guy to take it. But that same motorcycle wedged into a small, cramped gap between a wall and a house gives them much less room to go to work on your bike's security.

LOCK IT UP Well, duh. Of course you're going to lock it. But are you going to lock it up right? The next set of tips will tell you how.

30 LOCK IT OR LOSE IT

If you don't lock it up right, that lock may be worth less than the oil spot on the pavement that tells you your baby's long gone.

DOUBLE DIP Always use two locks. A big lock and an asymmetric, hardened, cut-resistant chain is the best, backed up by a U lock and/or a disc lock that can fit tightly around a wheel.

ANCHORS AWEIGH You need to lock your bike to something, otherwise the thieves will just pick it up or drag it off. Even if the bike is parked in your garage, you need a solid anchor.

WEAKEST LINK Chain your bike to a stop sign, and you may come back to find both sign and bike have done a vanishing act. Chain it to a steel

stoplight post and you're looking at better odds.

SLACKERS LOSERS Leave your chain or lock slack enough to reach the

31
PICK A LOCK

If you want to keep your bike, you need to get very aggressive when it comes to security. You should always use more than one method: Your handlebar lock, a disc lock, and a chain secured by a U lock are a good combination that's still portable. Keep locks and chains off the ground to deny thieves leverage, and consider an alarm and/or a kill switch in addition to active locking devices.

ground, and you might as well leave the keys in it. The ground means leverage: Get your lock up high and you gain an advantage.

LOCKS

	DISC LOCK	U LOCK

PLUSES	• Small. • Convenient. • Fast.	• Easy to carry in your backpack. * Sometimes fits under the seat. • Acceptably strong. • Cut resistant.
MINUSES	• A thief can lift the bike by the wheel and roll it away. • Risk of accidentally riding while lock is still in place.	• Some older U locks are easy to pick. • Bigger locks allow you to attach bike to a fixed object, but the options are limited.
	CHAIN	**CABLE**

PLUSES	• Unlimited number of locking options if chain is long enough. • Hardened, hexagonal chains are very tough to cut.	• Typically lighter than chains. • Like chains, thicker and longer is better.
MINUSES	• Thick, long chains are often heavy. • Only as good as the lock you use to secure them.	• Thick, long cables can be unwieldy. • Only as good as the lock you use to secure them.

32

PASS IN A TURN

Overtaking another bike in a turn can be tricky. Here's how to do it right.

STEP 1 Let the other bike know you're there—be sure he or she has spotted you before you make your next move.

STEP 2 Pass on the outside. This means a longer, wider line, but it's safer. The key is to accelerate well before you're parallel to the other rider.

STEP 3 Understand your line. The other rider may be on your ideal line, so you'll have to come in wider and maybe

exit wider as well. Never count on the other rider holding his or her line—they'll almost never close it up, but may run wider. If they do, they'll push you wider, too, so be ready for it.

STEP 4 Plan to overtake before or at the apex—that'll give you far more control on the exit. If you've carried more speed into the corner for the pass, you should easily out-accelerate the other rider from the apex to the exit.

33 PICK THE PERFECT LINE

When motorcyclists talk about "line," they don't mean something you use for fishing. They're talking about the exact path their bike travels over a road or track. Each line has three parts: the entry, the apex, and the exit, and a line is usually described as having an early or late apex. In addition to the illustration here, a great way to visualize line is to visit a racetrack and look at the darker area on the track surface, where the bikes have laid down rubber from their tires.

Most new riders begin their turns too soon and go into an early apex, which forces them to run wide on the exit. Entering the turn wider and waiting later to make the apex may seem counterintuitive, but it's usually both

safer and faster. You can see farther through the turn, and at the turn's exit you'll find you have much more road to work with.

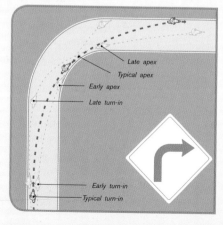

34 PASS A CAR SAFELY

Ride often enough and you'll come to view moving cars as dangerous, rolling roadblocks. Motorcyclists have two great advantages over automobiles—acceleration and maneuverability. Smart riders use both to their best interests.

BE DECISIVE Overtaking should be done as quickly as is safe. When ahead of or behind the car, you're relatively safe, but when you're beside the other vehicle you're vulnerable and have fewer collision-avoidance options. Don't speed up when you've pulled beside the car; instead, make the decision to pass, indicate, and then begin to accelerate while you're still far behind the vehicle. Downshifting allows your bike to accelerate faster, but you don't want to have to upshift in the middle of your pass. Choose a gear that's low enough

for aggressive engine response but that still lets you finish the pass.

BE AWARE Avoid passing in intersections, and be extra careful in areas with lots of driveways or side roads on the passing side. Why? If the car wanders into your lane, runs wide, or decides to change lanes or pull into a driveway, you need to have a way out already in mind. When you begin your pass, look for an escape route if the car changes direction.

BE CAREFUL Watch the driver's mirrors and front wheels—these often hint at a turn a split second before the driver changes lanes. Be particularly careful if the driver seems distracted by things like texting or talking on the phone, eating, or other non-driving activities.

35 TAKE AN OBJECT LESSON

As riders, we've had to deal with some crazy items in the road, including a canoe, a flock of sheep, aluminum extension ladders, and 4,000 sausages. And that was just last week!

If you hit (some of) this kind of stuff in a car, you usually run over it. On a bike, you fall over. So don't hit it. Which means don't fixate on a target—instead of looking at that television set in the middle of the highway, look for a way around it. Use your motorcycle's maneuverability to avoid that junk. And don't presume that because something looks harmless, it's safe to run over it and keep rolling. That's car-think, and you're a rider, not a driver.

Also, don't follow behind vehicles with unsecured loads—when stuff starts flying off, it'll have your name on it.

36 RIDE ROUGH ROADS

Maybe there's some magical place where all the roads are smooth and the traction's perfect in every corner. If you find it, let us know; wherever we ride the pavement looks like it's been bombed.

POTHOLES These pits can do real damage to your tires and rims, and put you on your head, too. If you have to hit one, get your bike straight up and down, as opposed to leaning over in a corner. If there's a pothole right in your line while cornering, stand the bike up, cross over the pothole, and then lean over again and complete your turn. Stand up on the pegs dirtbike style, too—you don't need full leg extension, but get your backside off the seat.

ROAD SEALER Those black snakes slithering across the road are tar strips sealing up cracks. Adjust your line to miss them if you can. Avoid hitting them with your front wheel—crossing them with your rear isn't as bad. Downhills will be worse than uphills because of the weight on the front end. If the front does tuck, the sealer usually isn't very wide, so you still have a chance to save it.

PAINT Wet road-marker paint can be a real hazard. As with potholes, try to cross paint stripes with less lean angle than normal.

37 SWERVE SAFELY

One word: countersteering (see item #89).

Also, avoid target fixation. Look past the problem to your exit point. A safe swerve is made up of two parts: avoiding the object, and then recovering from the swerve to continue your path of travel. You can get some practice in a parking lot, using a small, soft object (like a paper coffee cup) as a pylon. Head for it, look past it, and countersteer around it. When you're on the road you won't have much time to react, so you need to make this an automatic response.

38 NEVER BUY A BIKE YOU CAN'T LIFT

In a world of hoary motorcycle clichés, this one deserves a place of honor. And yes, like many clichés of course it's true to some degree. You never want to be in the situation of having dropped your bike and being literally unable to get back into action. But here's the tricky part: You can probably lift a lot more bike than you think, using the techniques on the next page. If you're a person with some reasonable upper and lower body strength and you're not riding a bike that's as big as a barge, you'll probably be fine. Not sure? Find someone with a bike about the weight you're interested in, and ask if you can practice. Picking it up, that is, not laying it down.

39 RESTART ON A HILL

You've stalled on an uphill slope—what now? Don't panic; it happens. Just hold the bike up with your left foot, and use your the rear brake to keep from rolling backward; you can also put both feet on the ground and hold the bike with the front-brake lever. Now, it's time to get it started again.

Don't worry about finding neutral. Just pull in the clutch and start the bike in gear. Start to the clutch out before you release either brake. You'll feel the front suspension begin to compress—let it. As the engine begins to load, slowly release the brake while giving the bike plenty of gas. Get your feet back on the pegs as soon as you can.

Alternatively, you can just roll the bike back down the hill and restart at the bottom or while the bike is headed down. Both are easier if you can turn the bike around, and then go downhill nose first, which isn't usually an option on the street, but on the dirt it can be the easiest way to get the job done.

Just be sure to lean into the hill while you're turning, or you may take a wicked fall. It may even be easier to get off the bike entirely and stand between the bike and the hill.

40 GET BACK ON THE (IRON) HORSE

You've come to an unceremonious halt, and either fallen off your ride or dismounted in a hurry. First, make sure you're okay. If you're in one piece, the next order of business is to get your ride up on its wheels again.

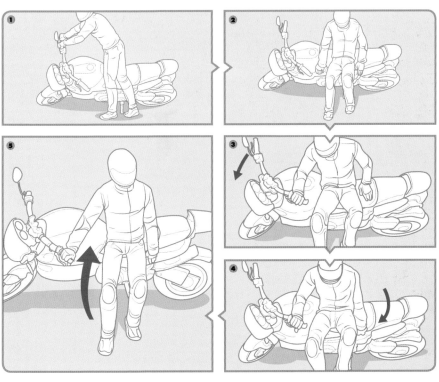

STEP 1 Kill the ignition, and make sure the bike is in gear. Turn the handlebar in the direction of the fall—if the bike's on its left side, turn the bar to the left. If it's on its right side, lower the sidestand.

STEP 2 Back up to the bike with your butt in the middle of the seat.

STEP 3 Squat down and reach for the handlebar. Hold the grip on the low side of the bike—if the bike's on its left side, then take hold of the left grip with your right hand.

STEP 4 Use your other hand to hold the frame or other sturdy part of the machine under or behind the seat, as low as you can get it.

STEP 5 Put your feet close together. Lift your chin and look up (to straighten your back to prevent injury). Now, push with your legs and your butt. Slowly take tiny steps back and walk the bike up. Once it's vertical, take care not to push it over.

Practice on a small dirtbike first. If there's anyone else available to help, ask!

41 UNDERSTAND STOPPING DISTANCE

Every basic driving course tells you there are two components to how long—and how far—it takes you to stop: reaction time and braking time. But motorcyclists need to know more.

A good sportbike can outbrake many cars, but not all motorcycles are equal in that regard. And more and more bikes offer ABS (anti-lock braking systems), a real benefit for most riders.

As speed increases, stopping distance increases a seemingly disproportionate amount. For example, let's say you're going 20 mph (32 kph), and it takes you 20 feet (6 m) to stop. Now let's triple your speed to 60 mph (97 kph). Tripling the stopping distance isn't accurate—in reality, you'll need more than 180 feet (55 m) to stop.

Of course the best way to know exactly how much road you'll need is to go out and practice—carefully.

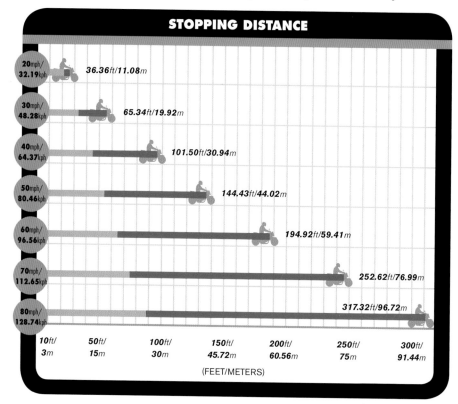

STOPPING DISTANCE

20mph/32.19kph	36.36ft/11.08m
30mph/48.28kph	65.34ft/19.92m
40mph/64.37kph	101.50ft/30.94m
50mph/80.46kph	144.43ft/44.02m
60mph/96.56kph	194.92ft/59.41m
70mph/112.65kph	252.62ft/76.99m
80mph/128.74kph	317.32ft/96.72m

| 10ft/3m | 50ft/15m | 100ft/30m | 150ft/45.72m | 200ft/60.56m | 250ft/75m | 300ft/91.44m |

(FEET/METERS)

42 MAKE AN EMERGENCY STOP

Despite your best efforts, you're boxed in, and there's no escape route. It's time to hit the brakes. You've just learned the math on reaction time and braking time, but in real life, riders need to know more. Here's how to stop safely and swiftly.

1. Get the bike straight up and down—you can't stop hard if you're leaned over.

2. Use both the front and rear brakes, hard. Up to 75 percent of your braking power is up front—using only rear greatly increases your stopping distance.

3. Shift your weight as far back as you can. You'll need to slide your butt back on the seat and push hard on the handlebar to keep from sliding forward.

4. If the rear wheel locks, go ahead and let it. Research shows that in a panic situation, those riders who released a locked-up rear wheel are also likely to release the front-brake lever, increasing stopping distance. Practice will show you that you can still control a bike with a locked rear wheel—learning on a dirtbike is a great help.

5. Be sure to pull in the clutch lever right at the start of this maneuver. Don't worry about using engine compression braking and downshifting in this scenario. If this is a real panic stop, you need to keep things simple and eliminate those variables.

43 HANDLE A SKID

In a car, you're taught to steer into a skid. On a bike, things are considerably more complicated. If your rear wheel starts to skid when you brake, the easiest solution is just to release the rear brake. But if you can't do that, here are some things to remember.

KEEP YOUR EYES UP Watch the horizon and where you want to go. The bike's natural tendency is to follow the front wheel. If the rear is loose, but the front still has steering authority and is pointed in the correct direction, you're in good shape.

SHIFT YOUR WEIGHT Putting more weight on the rear wheel may reduce the skid. Sliding forward, on the other hand, will probably give you more control by putting more weight on the front wheel—the one that's doing the steering, and not skidding.

GET ON THE FOOTPEGS Here sportbike, enduro, and dirtbike riders are at a big advantage because footpeg placement lets them "post" as on a horse—stand or weight the pegs to relieve the dead load on the chassis. You don't have to be fully standing, but getting the balls of your feet on the footpegs will give you and your bike better balance.

44 UNDERSTAND ABS

Compared to cars, bikes mostly have separate front and rear brakes. Motorcycles also use different front and rear tires; weight shift is another big part of your machine's stopping performance. Anti-lock brake systems for bikes and cars face different challenges.

ABS are relatively new for bikes. But they all work by comparing the front- and rear-wheel speeds; if one wheel is locking up under braking (skidding), it momentarily releases braking force and then re-applies it, up to 24 times a second. Many also apply both brakes, linking the front and rear. The front and rear brakes have some control over both wheels too.

ABS helps eliminate skidding, but does nothing for increased stopping distances on wet roads or ice. Since most riders tip over if they lock a wheel, anti-lock brakes are a real benefit. They're usually costly, add weight and complexity to a bike, and some riders resent the perceived loss of control.

45 DON'T GO TOO LOW

Imagine leaning through a turn and simply falling down on the low side of the bike—that's how the lowside crash gets its name. You may slide a bit, but since it's a short fall, your bones usually stay intact. The bike is also in front of the rider—good news, because otherwise it might slide over you.

Most riders think lowsides come from leaning over too far, but it's usually a loss of traction on slick roads, or caused by too much braking when leaned over. It can also happen if you tuck the front end with too much steering effort.

46 DON'T GET HIGH

A "highside" happens when the rear wheel loses traction, then regains it suddenly. Watch enough road-race videos and you'll see exactly what goes on—and

it's never pretty. When that big rear tire slips and grabs, it's enough to launch a rider right out of the seat, pitching him or her so high their feet end up higher than their head. A really bad highside flips the bike horizontal, a couple of feet above the pavement.

Most streetbike riders highside because they run a bike out of cornering clearance, lift the rear tire, and then a bump in the road causes the rear tire to regain traction. Or the rear tire spins under acceleration, the bike starts to slide, the rider closes the throttle suddenly, traction returns, and they go airborne.

How to avoid this? Once it starts, the highside is over in a split second. If the bike is leaned over and the rear wheel starts to slide, don't chop the throttle; it's better to lowside than have the bike hook up now.

47 RIDE IN THE COLD

In very cold weather your suspension oil may thicken, and your bike may ride harsher; your tires might also offer a little less grip on the pavement. These things are worth being aware of, but they don't really affect your ability to ride.

That said, unless it's actively snowing or you're trying to keep traction on an icy road, riding in the cold doesn't present any special problems for the way your bike handles—rather, your main concern is keeping yourself warm and comfortable.

A cold rider is going to have less coordination and longer reaction times. Motorcyclists make their own windchill, too. Winds of 60-70 miles per hour (95–110 kph) would make the top of the evening news, but on a bike, you experience that every day. So you need to remember three important things.

KEEP THE WIND OUT This means wearing windproof clothing (leather, textile) that seals tightly around your wrists, neck, lower legs, and waist. Boots and long gloves that overlap your pant legs and sleeves are a must. A scarf or neck gaiter can seal up your throat area.

KEEP THE WARMTH IN Several thin layers of insulation work better than thick ones. Even some folded newspaper shoved inside the chest of your jacket can make a noticeable difference in your comfort. Gloves need to be thicker on the back of your hands than on the palms.

GET WARMER Electric vests, seats, and handgrips can keep you warm even if your other clothing is marginal. And there's always that old biker favorite: a cup of hot coffee or tea to stoke the fires within.

48

SURVIVE A CROSSWIND

Few things upset riders as much as riding in a crosswind that pushes them around in a lane. Short of staying home or panicking every time it happens, here's what to do.

HOLD YOUR SPEED It's tempting to slow down when a gust hits, but that reduces your bike's stability. If you get hit by a gust, keep the throttle steady. That said, in windy conditions you should definitely slow down a bit, just not right after a gust hits you.

CROWD THE SIDE OF THE ROAD If the wind is blowing from right to left, crowd the right side of the road. You'll seldom overcorrect into the wind, but you'll have more lane to work with if the wind does move you.

HANG OFF INTO THE WIND Shift your body lower and into the wind to compensate for its effect. Hunching over also reduces the sail effect your body presents.

READ THE WIND As you scan ahead, look for blowing trees, grass, or dust in your path so a gust doesn't catch you unaware.

COUNTERSTEER Don't let the wind bully you; push back instead.

RELAX Don't tense up. Relaxing a little will actually help you react more easily.

49 PLAY IN THE SNOW

Riding in snow is a lot like riding in the rain, at least until the snow really starts to build up. While rain dampens every road surface, the real danger with snow is ice: It forms in corners where water runs off and then refreezes. It also forms faster on bridges, where air blows under and over the road surface. What to do?

GET KNOBBIES In some countries, you can buy special motorcycle tires. A dirtbike with knobbies will also work better than most streetbikes. If you're stuck and just need to ride a short distance, you can sometimes rig up ersatz tire chains by wrapping bungee cords around your rear tire—but be sure they clear the chain and swingarm.

FOLLOW THE TRACKS Stay in other vehicles' tracks—but only if they're fresh. If they're old, they'll ice up; you may be better off riding in the fresh snow next to them. Use more rear brake than front—this is normally the opposite of what a street rider would do, but riding in the snow is more like riding in the dirt.

WATCH THE LEVER In very deep snow, the stuff can upshift your bike when it presses up against the shift lever. You may have to ride with your foot on the lever to keep it down. When the snow gets much deeper than six inches (15 cm), it may be time to trade in your bike for a snowmobile.

50 GET YOUR BIKE WET

We've talked elsewhere about how to stay dry on a bike. Now we're going to talk about how to ride more safely when the road is wet.

Your biggest issue is reduced traction. Painted lines, manhole covers, and metal bridge gratings are real danger zones. Puddles may seem benign, but they can hide deep, sharp-edged potholes. If you see standing water on the road, pay attention.

Gentle control inputs are the key. You needn't ride significantly slower in the rain, but you won't be able to lean as far, or as suddenly. Easy on and off the throttle; ditto for the brakes. Take conservative lines—this is no time to dive for the apex. Try to be smooth, like you're giving your grandmother a nice ride on the back. Keep your brakes dry—

this means you'll have to drag them lightly every 3 or 4 miles (5–6 km), in order to heat them up and drive the water out.

It's smart to short-shift the bike (shift earlier to keep the engine revs lower) on the street, but do just the opposite (let the bike rev higher) on the freeway. Short-shifting helps keep the wheel from spinning at low speeds and lessens the torque multiplication at the rear wheel so the bike doesn't step out on paint stripes or manholes. Letting it rev higher on the freeway lets you use compression braking to gently slow the bike without depending on sudden brake inputs.

Finally, wear a full-face helmet. At speed, even small raindrops feel like little bullets.

51 ACCESSORIZE FOR THE RAIN

Two items can make a big difference in comfort and safety. The first is the "Biker Squeegee," which fits over your thumb and helps you keep your faceshield clean. The second is an anti-fog treatment for your faceshield or goggles—if you can't see, you can't ride.

52 BEAT THE HEAT

Planning to ride across Death Valley in July? Most modern bikes are pretty tolerant of hot weather, as long as you keep them moving so there's airflow over the radiator or cooling fins. Riders are a different issue, but there's plenty you can do to stay cool.

First, wear textile clothing instead of leather. You can wet it down, and the evaporative cooling of the windstream can keep you from overheating. Even better, pack some ice into your jacket's pockets—it will lower your temperature, and as the ice melts, it wets down the rest of your garments. If you do wear leather, look for a jacket with zip-open vents or perforated leather panels.

No matter how hot it is, keep covered up. A crash is just as likely when it's hot as when it's cold. Plus, long sleeves prevent the sunburn and windburn, as well as slowing your body's sweating processes, to help keep you from dehydrating. And bring a hat—when you remove your helmet you'll still need to keep your head cool.

53 SURVIVE IN THE DESERT

A breakdown in the desert is a real possibility for off-road or adventure riders. So what to do if you end up staring at a broken bike and a cactus? You should be with a friend who can pack you out as a passenger or tow your bike. On your own? You'd better get busy.

Heat, cold, and water are your main concerns, along with rescue. If it's the middle of the day, seek shelter (trees, brush, rock overhangs). No cover? Use a tarp, bike cover, or similar item to shade a small area.

At night, the desert loses heat quickly. Your bike provides lots of ways to start a fire—gas from the tank, oil from the engine, a spark from the plug or the battery. You can burn your seat, a tube, or a tire to make a smoky signal fire if there's no wood or brush. Your bike's mirrors, horn, and headlight are all potential signaling devices.

As for water: DON'T drink the coolant from your radiator. The best way to carry water on a dirtbike is probably a hydration pack, the biggest you can find.

Stay with the bike. If you must hike out, wait until the cool of the evening. Carry sandals or comfortable walking shoes with you; the inner booties from some motocross boots also give protection and are more comfortable to walk in than the boots themselves.

Your helmet will keep you warm at night, but it's a lousy hat during the day. Take a brimmed boonie-style hat with you or make one from a T-shirt.

54 CHOOSE YOUR COLORS

Ravens live in the desert, but they have black feathers. Polar bears lives in snow and ice, but they have white fur. Lighter colors should be cooler than darker colors, so what gives?

Loose fitting, dark garments (such as a raven's fluffed-up plumage, or a Bedouin's flowing caftan) are actually cooler than loose-fitting white clothes. If the garment fits close, the opposite is true. So keep your T-shirts and helmet white, and your riding suit dark.

55 BE A NIGHT RIDER

Riding at night offers two challenges: seeing and being seen. Bright lights, reflective clothing and helmet graphics, and even additional lights on your bike or person are the key. Bright colors aid conspicuity by day, but don't help much after sunset. A reflective vest is a good solution, as are reflective strips attached to a daypack, or as a graphics kit for many sportbikes. Flash your brake light to attract attention, and brake early to warn drivers behind you.

Your headlight needs to be in good order, and you may want to upgrade to a brighter bulb. But you also need a clean, scratch-free faceshield; ditto for your headlight lens. Consider adding auxiliary riding lights or fog lights if your electrical system can handle them.

You may have a fast motorcycle, but only short-range headlights—don't override them. And be particularly aware of wildlife at night—deer and other animals are most active at dusk and dawn, and often dart out into the road.

Use other vehicles' lights to your advantage—that truck ahead of you is illuminating a lot of road, and what he sees you can see—if you place yourself in the right spot and bother to look.

Remember, if you have to brake hard at night, the front end of your bike will dive, and consequently the headlight will dip too. Be ready to suddenly see less until you release the brakes—all the more reason to brake early and gently.

56 PARK YOUR STREETBIKE

When parking your bike on the street, roll it into the parking space backward, so the rear tire touches the curb. Leave your bike in gear so it doesn't roll. This is especially important if you must park it with the front wheel facing downhill.

Park defensively. It's better to be in the center of a parking spot than at one end where a car may try to squeeze in and knock your bike over. Share a space with other bikes if possible. There's power in numbers, and it conserves parking resources. Consider putting it on the sidewalk, but be aware that you might get a citation for that.

If you have to park on a hill, try to keep the sidestand on the downhill side. Try to park with your rear wheel facing downhill—it makes pulling out easier, and keeps the bike from rolling off the sidestand and tipping over.

If you're parking on a soft surface (dirt, grass, gravel) or brutally hot asphalt, put something under the sidestand to increase its footprint. A scrap of wood, a crushed soda can, a flat rock, a square of scrap metal all work—even something like a thick magazine folded in half.

In a public garage, utilize unused spaces where a car can't fit—behind pillars in parking garages, in wasted spaces next to elevators, etc. You will leave a parking spot open for a car, and doing so will also keep cars from trying to encroach on your space.

57 GET A ROOM

If you're traveling way (way) off the beaten track, you might actually be able to roll the bike right into your ground-floor hotel room, a common strategy when riding in Latin America (just remember to tip the maid extra if you leave an oil spot on the carpet).

58 TREAD LIGHTLY

Riding responsibly off-road means caring about your environment. It's the right thing to do. And if you don't, you'll soon find your riding area shut down and out of bounds. You can be a responsible rider by adhering to these guidelines.

BE RESPECTFUL Travel only on designated roads and trails or in permitted areas. Respect the rights of others, including private property owners and campers. Keep speeds low around crowds and in camping areas. If crossing private property, be sure to ask permission from the landowner(s), and leave gates as you find them.

MAINTAIN CONTROL On slick trails, moderate your throttle and minimize wheelspin. Ride over, instead of around, obstacles to avoid widening the trail. Yield the right of way to those passing you or traveling uphill, and give way to mountain bikers, hikers, and any people riding on horseback.

KEEP NOISE DOWN Less sound equals more ground: Make sure your bike has a quiet exhaust system and a spark arrestor. Avoid spooking livestock or any wildlife you happen to encounter, and be sure to keep your distance.

TAKE CARE Avoid sensitive areas such as meadows, lakeshores, wetlands, and streams. Leave the area better than you found it: Properly dispose of waste (and pick up litter left by others) and minimize the use of fire. Help to avoid the spread of invasive species, and restore degraded areas. Consider joining a local environmental organization.

59 KICK UP SOME DUST

The first rule for riding in dust: Don't ride faster than you can see. When you're out with a group, you can either stay close to the rider in front of you so his dust doesn't get a chance to rise (which only works if there are two of you on a wide trail) or ride at 30- to 60-second intervals, so the dust has time to settle. Standing up on the pegs can also help you see farther and over the dust.

Inhaling dust is bad for your lungs. A damp bandana over your nose and mouth helps. Even better: a dust mask from a hardware store, or a surgeon's mask.

Service your air filter after long dusty rides—if it gets too dirty, your bike will lose power and may ultimately suffer engine damage.

60 RIDE OVER A LOG

So, there's a fallen tree across your trail. Unless it's a sequoia or a redwood (in which case it's better to go around), it's time to rock some off-road skills.

STEP 1 Approach at a right angle, if possible.

STEP 2 Stand up on the pegs.

STEP 3 Just before your front wheel contacts the log, shift forward and/or tap the front brake to compress the fork.

STEP 4 Rock your weight backward, tug up on the handlebar, and open the throttle sharply.

STEP 5 Stay on the gas until the rear wheel climbs over the log.

STEP 6 If you can't get the rear wheel over, stay on the gas or stop and drag or lift the rear wheel over.

61 TRY A TRIALS BIKE

What is trials riding? It's about negotiating highly technical obstacles without putting a foot down. It's a way to improve your off-road skills by reading terrain, improving your balance, and finding out what your bike can do.

Pro-level trials bikes are specialized machines with minimal seats and tiny fuel tanks. Not ready to invest in one? Sign up for a school or visit a club in your area. You can even use a standard dirt-bike. It won't match a trials machine, but the next time you ride a trail with a terrifyingly steep dropoff on one side, you'll be glad you trained.

62 DUSTPROOF YOUR GOGGLES

Off-road bikes use foam air filters impregnated with oil to stop dirt from entering the engine. You can do the same with your goggles. Just put a little baby oil on the foam vents. They'll trap dust, and can be washed out with soap and water when the ride's over.

63 RIDE IN THE MUD

Off-road riding demands adjustments to the environment, your gear, and your skillset too. With these tips, you can avoid getting bogged down.

In the mud, you need to conserve momentum. Keep the bike as upright as possible and never slow to a stop. Don't be afraid of wheelspin as long as you're still moving—your rear tire may spin at 35 mph (56 kph) when the bike is only moving at a crawl, but if you're still mobile, that's all that counts.

Short-shift your bike to run it in a higher gear. Your riding position will probably be neutral or a little farther back, and you'll probably sit down more than when riding in sand. Slow down by throttle, or just use the rear brake.

Look for the high, dry (or drier) line. Mud riding is all about finding and using traction. Stay out of ruts, and maintain your balance on the bike.

Mud riding uses lots of gas and power. Even if it's soaking wet out, your bike can easily overheat in deep, thick mud, so watch your engine temperature. Just as in riding in sand, look as far ahead as you can, and stay on the gas.

64 PREP YOUR BIKE FOR MUD RIDING

Here's how to keep your bike running clean even in the dirtiest places.

Duct-tape under your fenders, airbox, and other spots where mud sticks. Coat undersurfaces and chain with non-stick cooking spray or WD-40, and consider running the chain looser, too. Stretch pantyhose over your radiator guards or oil cooler. Pack coarse, open-cell foam into gaps between the skidplate and engine, or between the brake lever and shift lever, and zip-tie it in place.

Reduce the tires' air pressure a bit in order to get a better grip in deep mud. Safety-wire your grips on.

Afterward, clean the bike *thoroughly*.

65 RIDE IN SAND

Before you even begin, lower your bike's tire pressure, especially on the rear tire. Depending on your specific bike and tire, this may even be as low as 12 psi (0.83 bar). Remove excess weight on the bike if you can–it makes riding easier, and picking the bike up easier still.

THROTTLE Sand respects confidence, aggression, and speed. Stop and you'll dig in. Don't fear wheelspin as long as you're making forward progress. It's tempting to let off the throttle, but sudden transitions are a bad idea here. Keep your revs up. As for brakes, you won't need them at all in deep sand. If you do brake, do it early, and gently. Get back on the gas as soon as you can.

BODY POSITIONING Unweight the front end as much as you can. That means lean back and keep your butt down, like you're trying to sit on the bike's taillight; you want to keep the front from digging in and to let it skim over the top of the sand.

YOUR LINE Front end starting to wander? Let it. With enough engine speed and bike speed, you can control the machine's direction with the weight of your feet on the pegs. The wagging handlebar can be unnerving at first, but you'll be fine.

Most important? Don't give up. If you're still moving, you're not stuck. When in doubt, and especially if you're getting tired, react with more assertiveness. If you do have to stop, wait for a patch of solid ground or a section with only light sand–getting restarted there is easier.

66
CARRY SPARE GAS

Lots of MX bikes only hold enough fuel for a half-hour moto. So what to do if you're out trail riding? The first solution is to get a bigger tank. Can't find one for your machine? Here are some options.

CAMPING GAS BOTTLES These containers hold up to one quart (1 liter), are rugged and easy to stow in a backpack, and seal well. Downside: not very much fuel.

TWO-LITER SODA BOTTLES Twice the capacity, half the durability—if that. Better than nothing, and readily available.

BLEACH BOTTLES Fill a basic 1-gallon (3.8-liter) bottle with fuel, and slip your belt (or backpack strap) through the handle to secure it. If the gasket in the cap is Styrofoam, replace it with a disc of rubber cut from an old innertube.

As soon as you burn through the first gallon (3.8 liters) in your tank, dump the bottle in—you'll minimize the time you have to carry its weight.

As for other, softer containers (like your hydration pack), don't even think about it. Note that carrying any extra fuel outside of your gas tank comes with a certain risk of self-immolation. Ride carefully.

67
RIDE WASHBOARD

Washboard or corrugated roads are created from vehicular traffic and the harmonics of suspension oscillation. Anyone who's ridden them knows they can be so bad that you chip a tooth, see double, or get hopped clean off the road itself if you ride them wrong. Here's how to float them like a pro.

DEFLATE YOURSELF First, air out your tires—you can go as low as 12 psi (0.83 bar). Stand on the pegs, or put at least an inch (2.5 cm) of air between your rear and the seat. Look as far ahead as you can while you ride, and vary your speed. Depending on the depth and frequency of the washboard ripples, you'll find a sweet spot.

GO FAST It's counter-intuitive, but riding faster is often smoother and offers more control than riding slower. Think of it as tuning a guitar, with twisting the throttle as twisting the tension key—you need to vary your speed until you find the right harmonic.

68 FILTER DIRTY GAS

Beggars can't be choosers, especially when the sun's setting, your bike is running on fumes, and the only gas available is sitting around in a questionable roadside steel drum.

Poorly stored gas generally presents three issues—rust, dirt, and water. None of them will do your engine any good, especially if your bike uses fuel injection. But there's hope: grab a piece of chamois (the split skin of sheep, used for drying cars after a wash). For decades, bush pilots have strained aviation fuel through a square of chamois to filter those troublemakers, and it will work for your bike too. Be sure you get real leather chamois, not a synthetic look-alike.

Another tool—especially if you know your fuel supply is questionable—is a fine nylon-mesh screen to fit into your bike's gas-cap opening. These are usually for fuel-injected motocross bikes, but you can adapt them to other machines. They won't stop water, but will catch most sand and rust.

69 GET IN A RUT

Riding ruts is like riding sand, but with one big difference. Sand riding is almost always on flat terrain, while ruts can be uphill, downhill, or flat.

Motocrossers use ruts as mini berms, but they can be trouble for casual riders. The key is front wheel control. Stand on the pegs and get your weight over the middle of the bike or near the rear wheel—it's easier uphill or on flats than downhill. Look ahead, not at the front wheel. Try to stay out of the rut. If the rear wheel drops in, stay on the gas, steer with the front, and ride out.

If the front drops in, use your tires' side knobs for control. Steer in the direction your bike wants to fall, and the knobs will grab the rut to help right you. Stay on the gas and ride it out. If both wheels are in the same rut, you can ride it out, or try to loft the front out and get the rear to follow.

If your wheels end up in different ruts, it's best to stop and drag the rear wheel into the same rut as the front.

70

RIDE FLAT TRACK

Flat-track combines the best of a track race and dirtbike riding.

THE SHORT VERSION
Gas it and turn left.

THE LONG VERSION
Flat track looks like a no-brainer; in reality it's one of the most valuable riding skills any dirtbike or streetbike rider can master. World champion road racers like Nicky Hayden, Kenny Roberts, and Colin Edwards all credit flat track for giving them the edge they need to win on pavement. Both Roberts and Edwards set up flat-track training facilities to share their secrets with other riders. Here are Edwards' Twelve Commandments.

1. Look in the direction you want to go.

2. Smooth inputs are key—slow on the gas, and gentle braking.

3. Minimize the time between brakes and throttle, which leads to finding neutral throttle. Crack the gas open before you're completely off-brake.

4. Throttle control keeps the chassis steady! Off-throttle to pinned is one smooth motion. Neutral is okay after opening the throttle; rolling off is not.

5. Elbows out for maximum control, and grip the throttle like a screwdriver, not a club.

6. Scoot forward in the turns, sit atop the bike, and hang that inside leg off for balance.

7. Compress the fork with the brakes and your weight to steepen rake and make the bike want to turn. In the dirt, use both brakes in every corner.

8. Push the bike down and keep your spine perpendicular and shoulders parallel to the ground; you're sitting on top of the leaned-over bike. (Body position in the dirt doesn't translate to road racing.)

9. Weight that outside footpeg!

10. Slow down in order to go fast.

11. Relax. It'll be easier to feel your bike.

12. Watch your tire pressures, but keep an even closer eye on your opponents' tire pressures.

71 RIDE IN SWAMPS

If you ride through a swamp, try to stick to the high ground wherever possible. Most dirtbikes have sealed ignitions and spark plugs, and high exhausts, but their weak link is the airbox—if your engine sucks in water, it will stall *right now*. Swamp riding means preparation.

Seal the airbox with duct tape, with just a small opening at the top. Your engine power is reduced, but it's better than having *no* power because of a drowned engine. If your bike has a carburetor, you'll need to run the carb vent hoses up higher too—under the top of the gas tank is a good spot. If the vent lines are submerged for too long, your bike will starve for fuel.

Keep your momentum up, run the bike in lower gear (more rpm), and try to stay balanced on the footpegs.

 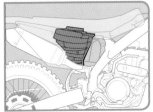

72 ROCK AND ROLL

Rock gardens and dry streambeds are often challenging, but they don't have to be. Of course, the size of the rocks makes all the difference.

SCOPE IT OUT First, stop and check out the section and your line. Pay particular attention to your entry and exit points.

KNOW YOUR LIMITS Be aware of your bike's ground clearance. If you get halfway and high-center on a rock, you'll be stopped cold. But if you know your machine has good clearance, you won't have to pass up an easy line due to a big rock.

STICK TO THE BASICS Pay attention to throttle control, balanced body position over the footpegs, and directing the bike where you want to go. Stand up in a neutral position with your knees bent and your chin up, looking at your exit. Keep the balls of your feet on the pegs. Keep your momentum up, and stay on the gas.

GET UNSTUCK If you do get stuck, try rolling the bike back as far as you can. Doing so lets you get your feet back on the pegs and regain your momentum for your next attempt. If you fall over, don't put your hand out to cushion your fall—it's a great way to break a wrist or a shoulder. If you know you're headed for a rocky section, you'll probably want to run higher air pressure in your tires to avoid pinch flats or bending a rim.

73 GET THE HOLESHOT

Ever been to a motocross race? The riders line up 20 or more abreast, all waiting for the start gate to drop. At the end of the starting straightaway there's only room for one rider at the first turn—whoever gets there first gets the holeshot. Achieving that requires clutch control, throttle control, and body positioning.

CLUTCH Your left hand has two jobs—to hold the grip and release the clutch. Use your index and middle fingers on the lever; grip the bar end with your ring and little fingers. Put the transmission in second gear. Let the clutch out almost to engagement. If the bike creeps forward, hold it back with the front brake.

THROTTLE While waiting to take off, hold the throttle at a high idle. At the starter's signal or when the gate drops, release the clutch and roll on the throttle at the same time. Once you've launched, hold the throttle open; if the bike wants to wheelie, slip the clutch only enough to control the front-end lift.

BODY Stand with both of your feet on the ground, keep your elbows out, and position your body well forward on the bike. Point the bike directly into the first corner. Look ahead to the first turn and watch for the gate drop with your peripheral vision. As the gate drops, lean forward into the bar pad to keep the front end on the ground.

74 STAND UP FOR YOURSELF

Over and over you've heard us tell you to stand up on the footpegs when riding. A motorcycle set up for proper control will have the footpegs pretty close to directly under your hips—dirtbikes are probably the best example, and cruisers with their pegs set way out in front probably the worst.

Think of all the active sports you've tried—tennis, baseball, soccer, even golf—keeping your balance is the first fundamental you learn. Same with riding a motorcycle. Along with your rear and hands, your feet are points of contact with and control of the bike.

Standing up on the pegs turns you into a dynamic part of your bike rather than just dead weight. It makes you an active part of the suspension. Off-road, it lets you see farther and above the dust.

For long distances, standing with your legs fully extended and your knees locked is the least fatiguing. In short sections, you can still "stand" even though there may only be an inch (2.5 cm) of air between your butt and the saddle. But compared to someone sitting down, you'll have more control.

When in doubt, or when you're tired, try these three things: stand up, give the bike more gas, and look farther ahead. Those are your "get-out-of-jail" cards.

75
MAKE SOME SPARKS

Nothing says hooligan like sparks flying off of your centerstand as you tear down the highway at night. Drivers will think it's the end of the world. Do it in front of cops and you'll get in trouble fast. And nothing is as much fun.

Going at a nice rate of speed, 30–60 mph (48–96 kph). Stay vertical, without leaning left or right. Then push the centerstand down with your left foot, hard! A huge stream of sparks will fly, and you'll laugh like a maniac inside your helmet. Do it enough and you'll discover the cost of replacing the stand. Which will be totally worth it.

76
BURN OUT THE DAY

The simple burnout is pretty safe and easy to do, but you will destroy your back tire, so consider whether there's a more eloquent and less costly way of saying, "Screw you, I'm outta here." Doing your burnout down a painted road stripe will be a little easier on your tire and produce more smoke.

STEP 1 Start in second gear, standing firmly on the ground. Pull in the front brake and the clutch all the way.

STEP 2 Ease the throttle to about 7000–8000 rpm, keeping the brake and clutch levers in.

STEP 3 Release the clutch, keeping the front brake fully engaged. The back tire will start to spin in place. The more throttle you provide, the more smoke you'll make.

STEP 4 Pull in the clutch, ease off the throttle, and ride off in a super-cool, carcinogenic cloud of tire dust and smoke.

77 MAKE YOUR BIKE BACKFIRE

Being tailgated by some brain-dead idiot who's texting and driving? Here's a sure way to get his or her attention.

STEP 1 Flick off your bike's kill switch. Not the ignition key, but the switch mounted on the right handgrip, which stops the spark to your bike's ignition. Be aware that your bike will slow suddenly at this time.

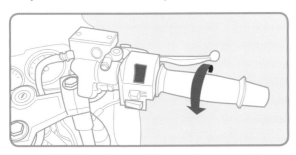

STEP 2 Hold the throttle wide open for two or three seconds, with the bike in gear. Gas and air will keep pumping into the exhaust and muffler system.

STEP 3 Flick the kill switch back to "run." Hot gases enter the muffler, and vapor in there ignites. This only works with carbureted bikes. And if you do it enough, you'll probably reduce your muffler to junk status.

78

DRINK AND RIDE?

In one word: Don't. In two words: Don't. Ever.

About half of the motorcycle deaths in the United States involve a rider who was drinking. A staggering 70 percent of ALL motorcycle accidents involve riders who have had a drink.

It's bad enough out there with all those distracted drivers eating hot dogs, texting, putting on makeup, and generally driving like a bunch of half-trained monkeys even on their best days. On the weekends, probably half of them have been drinking, too. Having a drink yourself on top of all that is just plain stupid.

Riding a motorcycle well is demanding. Most military pilots follow the 12 hours bottle-to-throttle rule. You should, too. And if you're on a date, it can make for a great excuse to spend the night.

79 POP A WHEELIE

There are three kinds of wheelie: the intentional wheelie, the unintentional wheelie, and the intentional wheelie gone bad. Here's how to do it right. The best bike to learn on? Someone else's, preferably a dirtbike. And wear all of the protective gear that you possibly can.

THE POWER WHEELIE Perfect for beginners. Sit back on the bike. Take off in first gear. When you're moving and the clutch is out, open the throttle quickly until the front comes up. Repeat this, trying to get the front end lighter and ride the wheelie farther. You'll learn throttle control and get used to the idea.

THE CLUTCH WHEELIE Start the same way that you would for the power wheelie, sitting back on the bike. Take off in first gear. When you're moving, pull the clutch in enough so that it slips. Rev the engine and let the clutch out until the front wheel lofts. Repeat until you can ride this wheelie farther.

Wheelie gone wrong? If the bike's starting to loop out, stab the rear brake and the front end will drop back down. It's always easier to wheelie with the bike pointed uphill. Sometimes, a small bump in the road or trail can help you loft the front wheel.

80 DO A STOPPIE

This is the wheelie's evil twin, sometimes called a nose wheelie. The first two steps (what bike to learn on, what to wear) are the same as for a wheelie, although a streetbike with a powerful front disc brake and a sticky front tire will work better.

Approach a flat, smooth area (parking lot, runway) and ride at 30–45 mph (48–72 kph). Lean forward to get your weight over the handlebar. A sportbike with a low bar is best.

As you reach the area that you've targeted, smoothly and quickly squeeze the front-brake lever until the fork is compressed. Then squeeze even harder while transferring your weight forward until the rear wheel begins to rise off the pavement.

Remember that you are not trying to stop the bike, just to get the rear wheel to come up. Once you can do that, try increasing your pressure and weight transfer until you can bring the rear wheel higher and higher.

Start out small. If a stoppie goes bad, all you can do is release the front brake, but there's a good chance it's all over. On the other hand, if it does go bad, you've mastered the endo.

81 SURVIVE A CRASH

No two motorcycle crashes are alike, but if you do kiss the pavement, knowing how to fall can make a big difference. Most important? The right gear (a jacket, boots, gloves and a helmet at the bare minimum). Back protector? Elbow and knee armor? Full leathers? You'll wish you had all of them in a crash.

First, get clear of the bike. Famous last words: "I can save it!" It's admirable that riders don't want to give up, but once the bike drops it's time to let go. Get a hand or a limb trapped between a sliding bike and the pavement and you're looking at a serious injury.

Keep your hands up if at all possible.

It isn't always (see the unlucky rider below), but do your best. If you're sliding, get onto your back and get your feet forward as soon as you can. Don't get up until you've come to a full stop. This may sound funny—how could anyone make that mistake?—but racers do it all the time. They think they're stopped, but they're not. They try to stand up and go flying.

Once you've stopped, get out of traffic as soon as possible, too. Logic dictates that you shouldn't move until you know nothing's broken, but you really don't want to be lying in the road and get run over.

82 HANDLE AN EMERGENCY

Maybe you've hit the ground. Or your friend has. But there's a rider down, and it's bad. The obvious action is to call 911. The best answer is to take some formal training before the incident—something that concentrates on trauma, the most likely form of injury a rider will encounter. Your local Red Cross is a great place to start, as are the local fire department and hospital ER; they can direct you to first-responder or EMT courses. In the meantime, you need a plan, and you'll need to execute it quickly. Remember the following, and it's imperative that you execute this plan in the following order: S-R-ABC-S.

SAFETY First your own, then the victim's. Accidents happen in dangerous places. Don't hit by another vehicle because you're too focused on helping the victim. Be sure basic safety is under control, then call 911 pronto.

RESCUE If the person is in a place where he or she needs to be moved to prevent additional injury? It's a no brainer. Otherwise, keep them still.

AIRWAY Be sure the patient's airway is clear. You can do this even if they're wearing a full-face helmet.

BREATHING The patient needs to be breathing. If not, consider CPR.

CIRCULATION Look for two things here—a pulse, and any life-threatening blood loss. Relatively minor blood loss can look terrifying; learn how to assess the difference between the two.

SPINAL Don't remove a patient's helmet unless you absolutely must—you might worsen any neck injuries.

Use every resource. Put bystanders to work directing traffic, calling 911 and so on. Take charge of the accident scene, and be sure nobody else gets hurt.

The first hour after an injury is most critical to treating injuries. If help is slow in coming, you'll at least have done as much as you can in that time. With multiple victims, use triage: Assess their injuries and prioritize their treatment accordingly.

83

PREPARE FOR A TRACK DAY

The street is no place to practice advanced sportbike skills—that's why you head for the track. Track and race days both happen on the same pavement, but track days are for improving riding, not winning a race.

BIKE If your bike isn't in top condition, you're wasting time at the track. Pay close attention to the tires, suspension, and drivechain. Do all the work before you go off to the track. Normal maintenance aside, most tracks will require specific bike prep—taping over or removing mirrors and lights, safety wiring oil drain bolts and filters, and replacing radiator coolant with distilled water. Check with the track beforehand for further instructions.

RIDER Visiting the track as a spectator is a great idea; attending the riders' meeting is a must. Getting your mind right (a track day isn't a race day) is a huge step forward. If you can, arrange a lap of the track in a car with you as an observer. You can also find "virtual laps" of some of the bigger tracks in various racing video games.

GEAR Most tracks require you to wear one-piece racing leathers (or a two-piece leather suit that zips together), a helmet, boots, and gloves. A back protector is a good idea, too. For short breaks you can just unzip the leathers; on longer breaks, shorts and sandals are welcome. If you don't own leathers, you may be able to borrow or rent a pair from a track school.

84
PACK FOR THE TRACK

Ideally, you'll go to the track with a friend who's familiar with the drill, but still, here are some pointers.

TRANSPORT Save the bike for the track. Team up with friends to save money to rent a truck or trailer.

COMFORT Bring a pop-up canopy for shade, and folding chairs. You'll be here the next eight hours. Also, take a cooler with water and snacks. Don't eat too much, but do eat something, and stay hydrated.

TOOLS & PARTS You shouldn't make major changes or repairs at the track, but take the basics to remove bodywork (for inspection) and to adjust the chain, chassis, control, and suspension. Extra brake and clutch levers let you keep riding after a minor tipover, too. Ideally, you should have your tires sorted before you head to the track; If you want to test other tires, have them pre-mounted on a set of spare rims.

OTHER ESSENTIALS Take about 10 gallons (38 liters) of fuel, a funnel and a fire extinguisher. 10- or 20-liter bottles are best. You'll need a swingarm stand at the minimum; a stand that holds the bike by the steering head is also a good idea. Don't expect electricity in the pits—get a quiet generator, some fuel, and a spare plug. And remember to pack a notebook to track what worked and what didn't.

85 DON'T BE THAT GUY

Remember, you're here to learn, not to be the fastest guy on the track. Guys who try to race you on track day are jerks—don't be one of them. Even if you're slow, nobody will laugh at you   as long as you're riding safely.

A common complaint about new riders is their failure to enter and exit the track correctly. When entering the track, follow the course marshal's directions. If you're going to exit the track, or suddenly need to slow, ride with your left hand off the bar and held up, and/or your right foot off the peg and held out. If you're heading to the pit, signal first, then slow down.

Definitely the number-one complaint is that new riders, out of misplaced courtesy, try to move over to give an overtaking rider room. Don't—just stay on the line you've been using. Unless you're actively trying to block someone, all the burden of passing safely lies with the overtaking rider. You should also remember to leave room when passing. This isn't a race, so there's no need to pass in a corner. Pass on the straights, and leave six feet (2 m) of room—most tracks are plenty wide enough.

Stay focused. The track is going to be a demanding and intimidating place. Getting tired? It's time to take a break.

FLAGS	WHAT IT MEANS
GREEN	Track is open for full-speed riding.
YELLOW	Caution; usually shown if there's a problem on the track. If the flag is waving, slow down and be vigilant.
RED	Stop. Usually you finish your lap, but at greatly reduced speed; check red-flag protocol for your track.
PASSING	You're about to be overtaken. Hold your line, but be prepared.
DEBRIS	Warns of oil or other debris on the track.
MEATBALL	Signal given to an individual rider. Pull into the pits.
WHITE	In racing, one lap to go. Crossed white and green flags (often rolled) means session is halfway done.
BLACK	Go to the pits immediately. Either you did something bad or there's a serious mechanical problem.

87 TAPE YOUR HANDS

Many dirt riders and some road racers tape their hands to avoid blisters when riding. Clean, good-fitting gloves are the first place to start, but with a roll of half- and one-inch (1- and 2.5-cm) medical adhesive tape, you can prevent almost any blister. Just follow this step-by-step guide.

STEP 1 Make sure your hands are clean and completely dry.

STEP 2 Cut out moleskin patches to cover up any areas where you have blistered in the past—usually the top of the palm where the fingers join the hand, but sometimes the inside of the thumb too. When in doubt, make the moleskin about twice the size of your last blister.

STEP 3 Cut a piece of tape 6 inches (15 cm) long; apply as shown. Repeat in any area where you get blisters.

STEP 4 Using the 1-inch (2.5 cm) wide tape, wrap a strip as shown, starting at the back of your hand and wrapping it over the palm. Press the tape down smooth and tight. Use two layers of tape.

STEP 5 Flex your hands. You want the tape tight, but not enough to restrict hand movement. Don't

use so much that you can't put on your gloves.

STEP 6 Dust talcum powder lightly on your hands or inside your gloves, to help you slide your hands into the gloves without balling up the tape. It will also help reduce blisters by keeping your hands drier and cutting down on chafing.

88 WARM UP YOUR TIRES

Motorcycle tires aren't just rubber—they're a complex combination of materials designed to work best at specific temperatures—typically around 165° F (74° C). But how do you get them to be that hot?

There are two ways: by using tire warmers, or by working the tires. The warmers are simple—you can think of them as electric blankets for your tires. Watch a Superbike or MotoGP race on TV and you'll see them on the bikes before they go out on the track—the racers get hot tires ready to go from lap one.

Not on the track? Then you'll have to do it old-school—by working the tire. Ride far and fast enough and the tire will come up to temperature naturally. But you can speed up the process with a series of progressively harder accelerations and stops. In the old days, riders used to swerve side-to-side as well, but testing has proven this to be ineffective.

Cycle World's Nick Ienatsch has a great approach: Ride on cold tires as you'd ride in the rain—be smooth, use authority, and make the most of your large inputs with the bike straight up and down—or close to it.

89 LAUNCH AT THE DRAGSTRIP

The standing quarter-mile (400 m) is the measure by which all serious streetbike engines are judged. A great time depends on a great launch. How to pull it off?

First, set your tire pressure right. Warm up your rear tire with a burnout: Hold the front brake, slip the clutch and spin the rear wheel. Start out in first gear, and get the engine up to peak torque—between 4500 and 9000 rpm.

Let the clutch out quickly while increasing engine speed. Rev up fast enough and the bike will start to do a wheelie; shift your weight over the front end to help keep it down. A little bit of wheelie is fine, but if the bike jumps up, you get wheel loft, not distance.

Another technique is to hold the engine rpm just below redline. Control your traction and speed with the clutch until the first upshift. The clutch will hate you, but the stopwatch will love it.

90 MAKE A PIT STOP

Endurance racers and Baja riders both need to make pit stops in competition. A fast road racing pit stop (two tires, full tank of gas) can be right around ten seconds; a dirtbike pit can take a minute or more.

KNOW WHERE YOUR PIT IS There's no shifting into reverse on a course if you blow past your pit.

BE CALM You shouldn't be in too great a hurry. Don't get tunnel vision—take in the big picture, especially if there are other riders pitting at the same time.

PUT IT IN NEUTRAL Coast into the pit. For a fuel-only stop, idle the engine; for tires, shut it down.

SIT BACK The fuel man will come in from your left. Stay on your bike but take your left hand off the bar, lean back, and give him enough room to work. While you're waiting, you can use that time to take a drink of water, polish your faceshield or change goggles, and get a brief race report.

EXIT UNDER CONTROL Off-road, you don't want to roost your crew, so get well clear of the pit before you dial up the gas. On a paved track, accelerate smoothly out of the pit, obeying the pit speed limit.

PRACTICE You and your crew both need to practice your pit technique. Smoothness counts!

91 DRAG A KNEE

Nothing defines modern road-race style like dragging your inside knee through turns. (Racing leathers with plastic knee pucks are a must.) This is less about your knee and more about your whole body. Keep your inside foot firmly planted on the peg through the turn—you want to weight the chassis hard. Now slide as far off the inside of the seat as you can while sticking your knee down and out, and moving your torso forward.

For a given speed and turn radius, you won't have to lean the bike over as far. Instead of leaning and then getting your knee down, do the opposite: assume the position, and then gradually decrease your turn radius (go in deeper), speed, and lean angle. Touchdown!

92 GET THE HANG OF IT

Motorcycles stop faster and accelerate harder when they're straight up and down, because that's when the tires put the most footprint to the road surface. Suspension components also work best in the pure vertical plane—leaning the bike over puts side loads on them, and encourages binding and frame flex. But we need to lean bikes over in order to turn. What can we do about it?

Hanging off on the inside of the turn reduces the amount we need to lean a bike for a given speed and turn radius. In each illustration below, you can see three red circles: one represents the center of gravity (CG) for the bike, one for the rider, and the third the combination of the two. There's little you can do about your bike's CG, but by hanging off you can move *your* CG (and thus the combined CG) lower and farther into the turn, so the bike won't have to lean over as far. In return, you'll have greater tire footprint and suspension compliance.

If you hang off far enough to actually touch your knee to the ground, you can also use your leg as stabilizing support to help hold the bike up in the turn. Naturally, this is an advanced technique only for racers, but even everyday riders can benefit from hanging off in turns, especially in rain or on poor pavement.

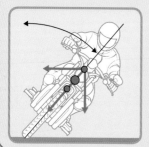

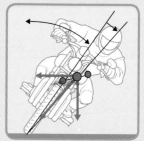

93 GET DOWN TO THE ELBOW

Wars escalate—what starts out as a little border dispute becomes an international confrontation. Same with racing: Mike Hailwood dragged holes in the outsides of his boots when he leaned his bike over in turns. Kenny Roberts and Jarno Saarinen dragged their knees. And now Marc Marquez, pictured here, drags his elbows. We have to wonder what's next—dragging your helmet?

When you combine such a body-to-the-inside style with the amazing grip of today's tires, there is no longer room under the machine for the classic knee-on-the-pavement position. Instead, you see today's riders packaging themselves along the bike: The inside knee is up against the bike, and the elbow is very close to the ground. All this is done in order to keep from having to lean the machine over any more than absolutely necessary. These days, really big lean angle numbers, like 63 to 64 degrees, are fairly common.

Many have noted that Marquez's bike is not leaned over as far as some. The reason is that his body is far off the inside to hold the bike more upright. And when he is ready to accelerate, he pushes the machine more upright very rapidly, putting it "on the carcass" instead of on the very edge.

94 PACK FOR A TRIP

Backpackers and motorcyclists soon learn that, as with so many things in life, less is more. The same goes double when it comes to packing for a trip. Some folks buy giant touring bikes, load them to tire-bursting capacity, and then hook up a trailer for good measure. Minimalists will take along a credit card, cell phone, and toothbrush, and probably cut half the handle off the last item. As for the rest of us, here's what we've discovered works for our trips.

GET YOUR PRIORITIES STRAIGHT
The bike comes first. Bring a small tool kit and some maintenance materials.

PACK RIGHT When you're shopping for luggage, buy small—it'll force you to pack light. Backpacks are the most versatile. Also, consider luggage designed for motorcycles, such as saddlebags or tank bags; they'll take the load off you and put it on the bike instead. When you do start actually packing, don't just throw stuff in.

Instead, put everything on the floor before you pack—then put half of it back. You may want to bring that stuff, but you don't need to.

PACK LIGHT Choose multi-use items. The pocket multi-tool (such as the iconic Leatherman) is a perfect example. Your bike cover can double as a ground cloth if you're camping, or your hammock might double as a bike cover. If you want to ride all the great back roads to that MotoGP race across the country, but you want to keep your bike light and nimble, then you can ship your clothes to the hotel via UPS, FedEx, or some other service. And remember, nothing is as compact or as versatile as cash.

SECURE IT ALL Bungee cords are your friends here. Motorcycles shake and move, and their loads compress and shift. Bungee cord elastic compensates; rope can't. If it moves and it shouldn't, use zip ties or duct tape. If it's not moving and it should, use WD-40.

95 GET A DRIVER'S ATTENTION

What with texting, phone calls, narcolepsy, and general ineptitude, automobile drivers may not be deliberately trying to kill you, but they can do a fine job of it without even trying. What's your best defense? First, you should get as far away from them as possible—especially from their blind spots. Second, be very conspicuous. In other words, let them know you're around.

SOUND Loud pipes? Some riders think they save lives. Not us—we've had too many idiots wake us up in the middle of the night blasting around on their loud ego enhancers. But loud horns? Big fan—we like them loud enough to have physical recoil.

CLOTHING Two words—bright colors. Especially your helmet. A bright construction-worker-style vest is an adequate substitute if you can't stomach a fluorescent pink jacket.

LIGHTS Blinking lights are best. A pulsating headlight may be legal in your area. And you can find bright blinking clip-on LEDs at any corner bicycle shop.

REFLECTIVITY The better riding suits and jackets incorporate large reflective areas. For helmets, you can apply reflective stickers. And that construction worker's vest will often have reflective patches, too.

MOVEMENT As predators, humans are hard-wired to spot movement. Droning along at the same speed as the cars around you makes you invisible. Moving in your lane, speeding up and slowing down and (best of all) passing the cars makes you more visible.

MIRRORS Don't assume a driver ever checks his or her mirrors, but position yourself where they'll see you if they *do* look.

96 FIND A GREAT ROAD

To my father, Interstate 5 was the eighth wonder of the world: wide, straight, smooth, flat, well-policed by Highway Patrol—and utterly mind-numbing. He lovingly called it the Superslab, and he droned along every bit of its 1,381-mile (2,223-km) length over and over with a smile on his face.

Most riders would call this a slow and painful lobotomy. The best bike roads are the opposite of a Superslab: They're light on traffic, picturesque, twisty, they gain and lose elevation, and they lead to a pleasant destination.

The old-school way of finding a good road is still a paper map. Avoid big straight lines; look for the thin, squiggly lines that wind next to those arteries, or snake along through uncharted lands.

Once a rider finds a road like this, he might share it with others. Plug in to a social network for riders, or a motorcycle website's forum. New to riding or new to an area? A local dealership may have riders who'll share a favorite road—or even organize monthly rides.

97 RIDE IN A GROUP

Want to be the Leader of the Pack, or at least a member? Keep these tips in mind and you'll be on your way to being a respectable participant in a group ride.

BE ON TIME AND BE READY If the group has to wait, then your ride may end before it begins. Be there on time with a full tank and an empty bladder.

HAVE A PLAN Who's leading? Who's navigating? Who's riding sweep? Does everyone have a list of everyone's cell phone numbers? Where will you stop for gas? What if someone gets a flat? Who has the tools? The first-aid gear? Does everyone know the route? What to do if you're split up at a red light? Do you all wait, slow down, or keep going?

RIDE THE PACE Group rides are a social commitment. If you can't keep up, drop out. If the group rides too slowly for your taste, ride with someone else. If you're a laggard or a speed demon, the ride will be miserable for you and the others too. Don't tailgate, either—no one likes a rider crawling up their tailpipe.

RIDE STAGGERED OR SINGLE-FILE On winding canyon roads, single-file riding is the smartest way. In town or on the highway, a staggered formation gives everyone room to maneuver. Riding side-by-side looks cool, but it's nowhere near as safe.

DON'T DAWDLE At gas or bathroom stops, get in and out quickly. Don't remove your helmet. Stay with your bike. Line up single-file at the pump, fill up, and roll your bike clear to let the next rider in.

SIGNAL YOUR INTENT If you're going to slow down or change lanes, let the other riders around you know what you're going to do.

CLOSE UP THE GROUP Spreading out too much is a number-one annoyance. Maintain some distance from the riders around you, but too much is as bad (and more common) than too little. A two-second rule—neither faster or slower—is probably right for most riding. In the dirt, riders string out on 30-second intervals to let the dust settle. When you come to a fork in the trail, wait until you can let the rider behind you know which trail to ride down.

IF A RIDER GOES DOWN Park your bike safely out of the road, and don't stand around in the middle of the road yourself. You don't want to get hurt, too.

98 LEARN COMMON RIDER HAND SIGNALS

Riding in a group? Everyone needs to know these common signals so you can communicate clearly and efficiently with each other. Need to give that rude driver a signal he or she will understand? There's always the extended middle finger.

STOP	SINGLE FILE
Arm extended straight down, palm facing back.	Arm and index finger extended straight up.

TURN SIGNAL ON	SLOW DOWN	DOUBLE FILE	FUEL
Open and close hand with fingers and thumb extended.	Arm extended straight our, palm facing down.	Arm with index and middle finger extended straight up.	Arm out to side pointing to tank with finger extended.

SPEED UP	HAZARD ON ROADWAY	REFRESHMENT STOP	YOU LEAD/COME
Arm extended straight out, palm facing up.	On the right, point with right foot; on the left, point with left hand.	Fingers closed, thumb to mouth.	Arm out 45°, palm forward, pointing with index finger, swing in arc back to front.

HIGHBEAM	COMFORT STOP	FOLLOW ME	PULL OFF
Tap on top of helmet with open palm down.	Forearm extended, fist clenched, with short up-and-down motion.	Arm extended straight up from shoulder, palm forward.	Arm positioned as for right turn, forearm swung toward shoulder.

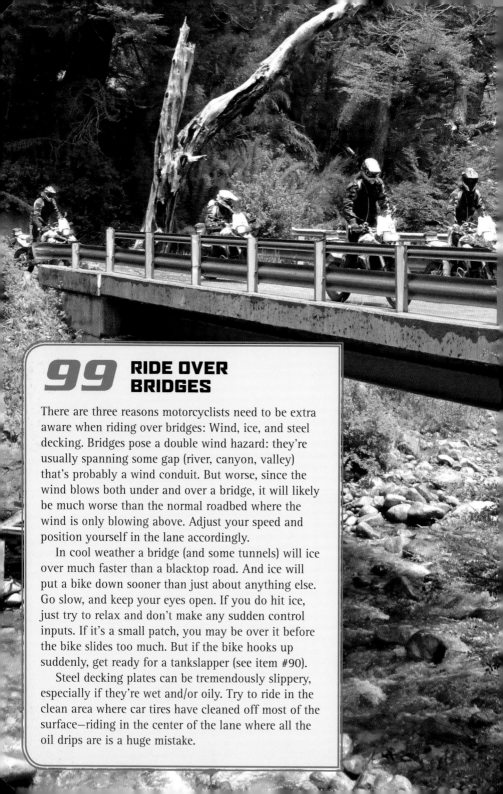

99 RIDE OVER BRIDGES

There are three reasons motorcyclists need to be extra aware when riding over bridges: Wind, ice, and steel decking. Bridges pose a double wind hazard: they're usually spanning some gap (river, canyon, valley) that's probably a wind conduit. But worse, since the wind blows both under and over a bridge, it will likely be much worse than the normal roadbed where the wind is only blowing above. Adjust your speed and position yourself in the lane accordingly.

In cool weather a bridge (and some tunnels) will ice over much faster than a blacktop road. And ice will put a bike down sooner than just about anything else. Go slow, and keep your eyes open. If you do hit ice, just try to relax and don't make any sudden control inputs. If it's a small patch, you may be over it before the bike slides too much. But if the bike hooks up suddenly, get ready for a tankslapper (see item #90).

Steel decking plates can be tremendously slippery, especially if they're wet and/or oily. Try to ride in the clean area where car tires have cleaned off most of the surface—riding in the center of the lane where all the oil drips are is a huge mistake.

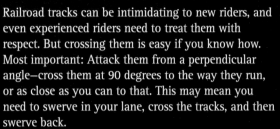

100

CROSS RAILROAD TRACKS

Railroad tracks can be intimidating to new riders, and even experienced riders need to treat them with respect. But crossing them is easy if you know how. Most important: Attack them from a perpendicular angle—cross them at 90 degrees to the way they run, or as close as you can to that. This may mean you need to swerve in your lane, cross the tracks, and then swerve back.

Stay on the gas while you cross them. Better still, slow before the tracks, and then gas it as you cross. Why? You'll lighten the front end so you maintain more steering authority, and the tracks won't grab the front wheel.

Finally, weight the pegs. You don't have to stand upright, but lifting your butt an inch (2.5 cm) above the seat turns your legs into a live part of the bike's suspension, and pushes your weight/contact point lower into the chassis (where the pegs join the frame). Keep a firm grip on the handlebar and look ahead. Congrats! You're safely on the other side.

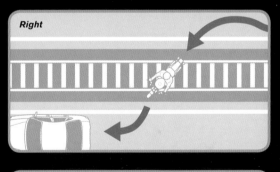

Right

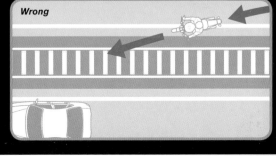

Wrong

101 RIDE WITH A SIDECAR

When it comes to riding with a sidecar, forget all you've learned about riding a motorcycle—most of it. When you hook a sidecar to a bike (and we're talking about traditional sidecar rigs here), the bike becomes a whole other animal.

Unless you're in the UK, Japan, or New Zealand, your sidecar will most likely be mounted on the right side of the bike. When you speed up, the combo will tend to turn in the direction of the sidecar; when slowing down, it will want to turn away.

Most sidecars have (or should have) a separate brake for the sidecar wheel linked to the rear brake of the motorcycle. Applying the rear brake will want to make the rig stop in a straight line—great if you're going straight, but maybe not so hot if you're trying to stop in a turn. Get your braking done in a straight line, whenever possible.

Within thirty seconds of your first ride, you'll find that you can't lean your traditional sidecar in a turn as with a bike. Forget countersteering, but do lean in the direction of the turn, as you would on a normal bike.

Sidecars handle best with weight in the chair. If you don't have a passenger, put as much weight as you can in the sidecar, and set it as low as you possibly can. About 50–100 lbs (23–45 kg) is good—that's about the weight of a couple of big bags of dog food. The worst thing you can do is ride with an empty chair and a passenger behind you.

Lifting the sidecar wheel in turns, known as "flying the chair" is an advanced technique that looks spectacular—as long as it's intentional. To practice, find a large, empty parking lot and ride some figure eights, starting out slow and gradually increasing your speed until the chair lifts. You'll immediately notice that you're now riding a large, unbalanced motorcycle that responds like a traditional bike.

102 TOW A TRAILER

Who says you can't take it with you? If you've jammed your saddlebags to the bursting point and still need to pack more gear, there's only one way to go: a trailer. They're popular accessories for long-distance touring riders, especially if they're travelling two-up and camping, but you should keep a few hints in mind.

USE ENOUGH BIKE You won't pull a giant trailer with a Vespa. Pick a bike that has enough power for the job—1000cc or more.

FILL YOUR TIRES The trailer puts additional load on both bike tires, especially the rear. Inflate them properly, on the upper end of your bike's GVWR.

HITCH IT RIGHT Your bike needs to lean into turns, but the trailer doesn't lean. You'll need a hitch that lets the trailer both turn and swivel—think about how a U-joint works.

FIND YOUR PLACE Trailers are almost always wider than a bike, so you'll need to ride closer to the center of the lane than you would without a trailer. You'll also be riding closer to the center-of-the-lane oil slick you'll find on most roads, so exercise caution.

STOP THAT THING Trailers increase both a bike's weight and its stopping distance. They also want to overrun the bike when it's stopping unless the trailer is equipped with its own set of brakes. Ride with caution, use brakes early and carefully, and give yourself plenty of stopping room.

FIND PARKING Your motorcycle-and-trailer rig is much longer than your bike alone, so you need to scout out an appropriate parking spot. Fine one that will let you pull straight out when leaving. Bikes are agile; towing trailers, not so much.

103 RIDE AROUND THE WORLD

Who hasn't looked at a motorcycle, and thought how much fun it would be to chuck it all and ride around the world? Plenty of people have: just check out accounts like Helge Pedersen's *Ten Years on Two Wheels* or Ted Simon's classic *Jupiter's Travels*. You can do it, too—if you want it bad enough.

Much of the world—at least the interesting parts—hasn't been paved (yet), so you'll be riding on dirt roads. You don't need a full-on motocross bike, but a single-cylinder of at least 650cc like the timeless Kawasaki KLR650, or a twin like the KTM990, BMW 1150 or 1200 GS are all proven choices. The great German aircraft designer Kurt Tank outlined four key attributes necessary for military equipment: It needs to be simple, robust, reliable, and easy to maintain. The same guidelines apply to your round-the-world bike.

It's easy to overload your bike, so do like Pedersen recommends and fit your bike with small panniers. Nature (and

your panniers) abhors a vacuum, and you'll end up filling whatever you have. Almost all serious round-the-world riders choose some sort of aluminum-box pannier for the winning combination of security, capacity, and weather resistance. A tank bag and a cargo rack give you additional storage room, but remember, you're just going to the next place where you can buy gas, not to the moon.

Bring a change of clothes, everything you need to repair multiple flat tires, GPS and paper maps, and paperwork: passport, driver's license/permits, visas, registration, proof of ownership, and Carnet de Passage en Douane (a temporary bike import document).

As for the cost . . . well, how much do you have? $20,000 is probably a good working budget for gas, freight, and the basics, and of course the price goes up from there. Best currencies to bring? The US dollar and the Euro; in Africa you can add the British pound, too.

104 KNOW YOUR DOCUMENTS

You know how all those war movies have the uniformed officer with a clipped accent asking for your papers? It won't be quite like that, but you should be sure you have everything in order.

INTERNATIONAL DRIVER'S LICENSE Most European countries will honor your home driver's license (as long as it has a motorcycle endorsement), but it never hurts to also have an international driver's license. Your local motor vehicles department or automobile club can usually arrange one.

INSURANCE You may be able to take care of a policy through your insurance company back home. If you're with a tour, they'll probably handle everything. Frequent travelers could join a local auto club, like Germany's ADAC, which offers comprehensive insurance packages, including medical transportation.

HIGHWAY TAX Note that in some countries (especially Switzerland) you'll need to purchase a "vignette," a small decal to show that you've paid to use the country's highway system. You can purchase them in advance or at the border in the customs office.

105 RIDE LIKE A NATIVE

Riders from elsewhere need to learn to read European road signs in advance. You'll be riding fast, and some won't be immediately intuitive. You'll reduce your risk of getting confused or lost if you study up in advance.

In Europe, lane etiquette means staying in the right lane unless you're passing. Pay attention to your mirrors. Respect car drivers, and be aware of regional differences. In Italy, for example, the horn is used frequently. In Germany, a driver signals irritation with a flash of their headlights—if you get honked at instead, you did something *really* bad.

Finally, most of the speeding tickets issued in Europe are from remote radar cameras—you can get four or five in a day without even noticing. If you see a bright light flash, prepare to open your wallet.

106 TAKE THE TOP 10 RIDES

Everyone has their favorite rides, but this list of locales is hard to beat.

ALPS AND DOLOMITES Hairpin turns, gorgeous vistas, and great food make this entire region a no-brainer. The great mountain passes of the Tyrol region have no equal.

CHILE/PATAGONIA The west side of South America is a world unto itself. Wherever mountains tumble down to the ocean like this, the roads twist and turn—a rider's dream!

RIO AND REGION The ride between Rio and Sao Paulo is an amazing 900-plus miles (1,450 km) from the coast of Brazil through the country's awesome mountains.

CÔTE D'AZUR The famed French Riviera, on the Mediterranean's north edge, offers beautiful scenery, great roads, and wonderful food.

ROME AND ITS ENVIRONS The Roman road system has been one of the best in the world since antiquity. These days, you get also get rugged topography and legendary cuisine.

CAPE TOWN TO JO-BURG South Africa is one of the easiest destinations on the big continent, and this ride is one of the best. You'll see it all—ocean, grasslands, and mountains.

AUSTRALIA'S EAST COAST From Melbourne to New South Wales to Queensland, this Pacific-coast route means surfing and easy cruising along with more demanding twisties.

SOUTHERN NORWAY This underappreciated motorcycle destination offers lots of gorgeous and challenging terrain, easily enough for two weeks' worth of riding.

NEW ZEALAND A rider's paradise thanks to the roads and terrain—and people. Christchurch to Auckland makes for a grand trip.

CALIFORNIA'S PACIFIC COAST The ride from San Francisco to Malibu is best, and you can stop for the MotoGP races at Laguna Seca.

107 EXPLORE BAJA

A thousand miles (1,600 km) long, stretching from the California border down to Cabo San Lucas, Baja is an incredible place to ride.

You can ride pavement down the entire length of the peninsula. But to really get the most out of the experience, you'll want to take a machine you can ride on dirt roads. And don't even worry about bringing a bike with a license plate—a pure dirtbike will do. So will big single-cylinder dual-sport or a twin-cylinder adventure bike.

What to bring? First off, plenty of tire-repair materials. If you're riding on a dirtbike, consider upgrading to a bigger "desert" tank, at least four gallons (15–16 liters). Never pass up gas when you get the chance to fill it. Gas stations are easy to find, but you may have to travel a ways between them. And take a spare air cleaner too—you'll need to service it every night due to Baja's dust, especially in the summer off-road. As for navigation, you won't need more than an AAA map, although a GPS is always worth packing.

If you go to Mexico, you will have to have proof of ownership for your bike. And don't even think about bringing in guns or illegal drugs.

When to go? Well, it's hot in the summer and cold in the winter. The winter and spring are best for the east coast where it gets humid, the summer for the higher central spine, and the summer and fall for the Pacific coast.

108 RIDE THE LONGEST HIGHWAY

The Pan-American Highway is the most direct north/south route through Central America. Depending how one defines it, it runs from Prudhoe Bay above the Arctic Circle all the way down to Ushuaia at the tip of South America. By the most generous definition, you can cover close to 30,000 miles (48,000 km). The "official" route starts in Monterrey, Mexico and concludes in Buenos Aires, Argentina.

If you're thinking of an eight-lane Autobahn, think again. Most of the Pan-American is paved, but 50 miles per hour (80 kph) is about the maximum speed. And it will be mostly two lanes.

A notable missing link is the Darién Gap between Panama and Columbia, a 99-mile (160-km) section of mudfest and swampland that's defied pavement. The truly adventurous will try to battle through this area, while mere mortals will jump the gap by ferry.

109 SURVIVE LATIN AMERICA

Latin America (from Mexico all the way down to the bottom of South America) is one of those great underappreciated travel destinations for motorcyclists. One language (Spanish) will get you through almost all of it (and while not ideal, you can manage most of Brazil with it, too). The area encompasses more than 7 million square miles (18 million square km) and about 15 percent of the world's landmass, so there's plenty to explore. It's affordable, there are vast areas of nature to experience, and most regions are bike friendly and bike savvy. There's just enough infrastructure to provide support, and in general the governments are reasonable to deal with.

Riding in Latin America is tremendously rewarding, and for the most part the people are unusually friendly. But the countries do vary widely, and can change from year to year. Some can become war zones between drug cartels, governments, rightist paramilitaries, and leftist guerillas. Others (notably Costa Rica) are so peaceful the country doesn't even have an army.

As for motorcycles, a solid adventure-touring bike is probably you best choice here, although most streetbikes will make the trip. You can camp, but accommodations in Latin America are generally affordable and let you lock your bike up safely at night—theft is an unfortunate but real issue.

110 EXPERIENCE VIETNAM

The best way to see Vietnam is by bike, and there's plenty to see. There's enough infrastructure to make this trip doable, the weather's warm year-round, and a bike is the chosen form of transport for the locals.

Honda's world-famous C90 Cub may be all you need—a 250 twin is the biggest bike you'll want. The bureaucracy of travel permits and bike importing will need patience; you can also rent or buy a bike instead.

Traffic may seem crazy, but embrace the chaos and go with the flow. Prepare to deal with unimproved roads—again, a native bike is the best choice: the locals know what works. Monsoon season is legendary—November to February is the coolest and driest time.

111 RIDE LONG (NO, REALLY LONG) DISTANCES

Every two years, the aptly named "Ironbutt" race takes place in the U.S over eleven days and 11,000 miles (17,700 km). Riders must hit a series of checkpoints in a very tight timeframe. Why does this matter to you, if you never plan to subject yourself to this kind of fun? Well, these folks know about surviving a really long ride. Here are some of their key hints.

KNOW YOUR LIMITS If the longest you've ever ridden is 250 miles (400 km), don't plan on a string of 1000-mile (1600-km) days. Then, try to eliminate all irritants. Something that's a minor annoyance can finish you off after that great a distance.

BE PREPARED Prepare your bike before the trip. We're all short of time,

but if you can't get your bike right before you start, on the road is no place to try and make repairs. Don't make any big repairs or changes (accessories) just before the trip. Upgrade your tool kit . . . and join a towing service, just in case.

BE SAFE Forget about high speeds. Slow and steady wins this race. And really, really, really forget about drugs. Not even coffee. If you're tired, stop. Get into your rain suit before it starts raining. Get gas before you need it. Never ride faster than you can stop. Stay away from long-haul trucks.

GEAR UP Pack wisely. Less truly is more in this race. Keep the things that you will need easy access to (flashlight, eyeglasses) in a tank bag where you can reach them with a minimum of trouble.

Do make some room for an electric vest, though. Carry a flat-repair kit and know how to use it.

REST RIGHT Know when it's time to stop. Getting tired? Pull over now! And remember, it's often the case that a rest stop can make you go faster.

BE HEALTHY If you can't eat right, at least eat light. Be sure to stay hydrated, and when outside of well-populated areas, carry at least a half gallon (2 liters) of water. Carry vitamins and aspirin, too.

BE AWARE Be careful crossing county lines. Road maintenance can change quickly when one county runs out of money. That nice two-laner can become a potholed mess within moments.

CROSS AFRICA

This is the ultimate adventure-bike destination. In the north, you have the Sahara desert to contend with. Below that the continent has a full catalog of animals who are happy to eat you. Snakes like the mamba are fine with killing you just for sport. Even a mosquito or tsetse fly can take you down.

If you want a beginner's route, choose South Africa. It's easy, and you can be out in the bush country while just a short ride from major towns.

Tanzania, Uganda, and Kenya offer great wildlife viewing and plains riding. Morocco blends African and Arabic influences, and Algeria, Libya, and Tunisia return the classic Sahara experience. And nothing compares to Egypt.

The first traditional trans-African route runs from the Mediterranean south to Cape Town, generally along the west coast. The second runs from Cairo through Sudan and Ethiopia, to Kenya, and south from there. At the time of this writing, Sudan is politically unstable, and stability is worth mentioning for any African country. It's a big continent, and there's no reason to take risks when there's so much to see. Treat unstable nations like potholes: Ride around them.

113 NEGOTIATE ROUNDABOUTS

The first time I ever rode in Rome, it was at night, in the pouring rain, and I was following a local who rode like a madman. I had no idea where I was going, didn't know our hotel's name, and if I lost him, I was finished. So I stood up on the pegs, pinned the throttle, and rode the way I'd ride a motocross bike. When in Rome . . .

When negotiating any roundabout, traffic circle, or developing-world intersection, just dive in and go for it.

Use your bike's biggest advantages to their fullest: maneuverability and acceleration. If you overshoot the turn, keep going and try again.

This is no place for the timid; ride with conviction. Hand signals and blinkers are often ignored; the only escape is to ride faster than whatever is trying to run you over. Don't stop or slow down. It's like being in an avalanche—keep moving, stay on top, and you'll be fine!

114
CARRY A
LIVE PIG

There are two proven methods. In both of these cases, however, one major hint applies—avoid both ends of the pig. One end has sharp teeth, and pig effluvium is probably the most vile substance in the world.

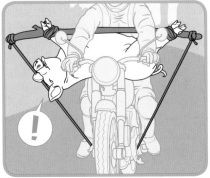

POLE METHOD Tie the pig to a bamboo pole, cannibal style (with the forefeet and hind feet tied together, and with the pole slid through the gap between the legs and the feet). Secure pole crosswise over the bike's chassis. This idea works best if you keep the pig in the step-through area between the seat and the handlebar.

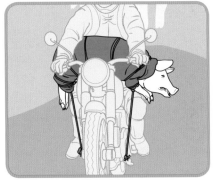

WRAP METHOD Wrap the pig in something (a blanket, fish net, or chain-link fence section). Tie securely. Lay pig on lap, and tie each end to a footpeg. Alternately, you can lay the trussed pig on the seat, and sit on top of it.

INDEX

PHOTOGRAPHY CREDITS

ILLUSTRATION CREDITS

CYCLE WORLD

Executive Vice President Eric Zinczenko
Editorial Director Anthony Licata
Publisher Andrew Leisner
Editor-in-Chief Mark Hoyer

Cycle World and Weldon Owen are divisions of **BONNIER**

Library of Congress Control Number on file with the publisher

ISBN 13: 978-1-61628-675-0
ISBN 10: 1-61628-675-X

10 9 8 7 6 5 4 3 2 1

2013 2014 2015 2016

Printed in China by 1010

weldon**owen**

President, CEO Terry Newell
VP, Publisher Roger Shaw
Associate Publisher Mariah Bear
Editor Ian Cannon
Creative Director Kelly Booth
Art Director Meghan Hildebrand
Illustration Coordinator Conor Buckley
Production Director Chris Hemesath
Production Manager Michelle Duggan

All of the material in this book was originally published in *The Total Motorcycling Manual* by Mark Lindemann.

Weldon Owen would like to thank Allister Fein and William Mack for the original design concept for *The Total Motorcycling Manual*.

© 2013 Weldon Owen Inc.

415 Jackson Street
San Francisco, CA 94111
www.weldonowen.com